Poptropica® English

STUDENT BOOK 6

Future Island

José Luis Morales • Laura Miller • John Wiltshier
Series advisor: David Nunan

Pearson Education Limited
Edinburgh Gate
Harlow
Essex CM20 2JE
England
and Associated Companies throughout the world.

Poptropica English

© Pearson Education Limited 2015

Based on the work of Aaron Jolly

The rights of John Wiltshire and José Luis Morales to be identified as authors of this work have been asserted by them in accordance with the Copyright, Designs and Patents Act 1988.

Stories on pages 16, 28, 40, 52, 64, 76, 88, and 100 by Catherine Prentice. The rights of Catherine Prentice to be identified as author of this work have been asserted by her in accordance with the Copyright, Designs and Patents Act 1988.

Phonics syllabus and activities by Rachel Wilson

Editorial, design, and project management by hyphen

All rights reserved; no part of this publication may be reproduced, stored in a retrieval system, or transmitted in any form or by any means, electronic, mechanical, photocopying, recording, or otherwise without the prior written permission of the Publishers.

First published 2015

Eleventh impression 2020

ISBN: 978-1-292-09136-5

Set in Fiendstar 13/16pt

Printed in Slovakia by Neografia

Illustrators: Illias Arahovitis (Beehive Illustration), Leo Cultura, Mark Draisey, Michael Garton (The Bright Agency), John Haslam, Ned Jolliffe (Eye Candy Illustration), Moira Millman, Ken Mok, Zaharias Papadopoulos (hyphen), Rui Ricardo (Folio Art), Christos Skaltsas (hyphen) and Olimpia Wong.

Picture Credits: The Publishers would like to thank the following for their kind permission to reproduce their photographs:

(Key: b-bottom; c-center; l-left; r-right; t-top)

123RF.com: 12/5, 74 (i), 104r, Arvind Balaraman 70 (Samir), Cliff Dabbs 36/3, Marina Gallud 74 (b), Eric Isselee, 24/12, jianfei su 32/1 (b), Karina Manams 87/3 (b), Cristi Matei 89/4, Martijn Mulder 17/5 (suntan lotion), Jatesada Natayo 27cl, Denis Radovanovic 54 (b), Paul Simcock 46bl, Eddie Toro 106/1, Ales Zvolanek 91 (b); **Alamy Images:** amana images inc. 95b, Art Directors & TRIP 91 (a), 91 (d), 91 (f), David Ball 43/5, Thomas Cockrem 71b, Cotswolds Photo Library 43/3, Danita Delimont 31 (above centre), Flirt 26 (h), Oliver Gerhard 30r, Paul Harrison 55b, Nigel Hicks 55t, Mike Hill 32/3 (c), Image Source Plus 38 (e), IML Image Group Ltd 23 (b), Arif Iqball 94 (b), Juice Images 94bl, Kuttig - Travel - 2 42t, Keith Levit 31 (below centre), Loop Images Ltd 43/4, Mode Images 12/7, Carlos Mora 95 (c), N. Reed of QED Images 36/6, Barrie Neil 19l, 19r, David Pearson 36/7, Pictorial Press Ltd 91 (e), Chris Rout 70 (Zara), Alex Segre 36/8, Shorelark 55c, Ken Welsh 46 (b), Henry Westheim Photography 62/6, Chris Willson 94 (a); **Digital Vision:** 87/2 (a); **Fotolia.com:** 2xSamara.com 38 (b), Africa Studio 17/5 (insect repellent), Anatolii 26 (e), Leonid Andronov 38 (d), Galyna Andrushko 17/3, antonsov85, 17/4 (pasta), atoss 10 (c), Arvind Balaraman 78, banepetkovic 17/1, Lance Bellers 36/9, Samuel Borges 81l, Alex Bramwell 24/9, bst2012 23b, chrom 26 (c), Dhoxax 66 (a), dreambigphotos 48/6, dule964 26 (i), Andriy Dykun 24/11, Ericos 24/13, 26 (d), Fotos 593 60/6, Foxy_A 43/1, Vladislav Gajic 103 (d), Gelpi 89l, 90, golandr 17/4 (tin cans), Jörg Hackemann 62/3, hatchapong 62/5, Dieter Hawlan 46 (a), helgidinson 60/2, HLPhoto 48/5, huci 103 (b), ia_64 17/5 (torch), igor 27bl, iofoto 67/3, Eric Isselée 24/3, 24/8, ivanukh 60/5, J and S Photography 17/5 (gas stove), jahmaica 103 (a), JJAVA 48/10, jobhopper 36/2, k_vladimir 89/3, karnizz 60/4, Cathy Keifer 31b, Veniamin Kraskov 12/2, Artur Marciniec 48/7, Nataraj 62/2, nemar74 103 (e), Duncan Noakes 27cr, Tyler Olson 38 (f), Didier Ritzmann 22 (a), rnl 32/4 (a), robertkoczera 12/6, Jérôme Rommé 32/2 (b), Jarosław Roś 60/3, Rui Vale de Sousa 51, Sabphoto 42c, Ruta Saulyte 43/2, Elena Schweitzer 10 (d), 74 (d), shaunleephoto 32/3 (b), silver-john 71 (c), Janis Smits 17/5 (matches), sombra_de_luna 24/7, StarJumper 24/10, franck steinberg 32/4 (b), stuartbur 48/11, sumire8 60/1, swisshippo 31t, Ali Taylor 67/2, Tiramisu Studio 48/1, tycoon101 48/2, Dmitry Vereshchagin 74 (h), vichie81 47 (c), Viktor 48/3, Richard Villalon 12/9, vitalliy 62/1, volga1971 24/1, wittybear 87/4 (b), Brad Wynnyk 89r, xalanx 53; **Getty Images:** Esbin-Anderson 54 (a), Haven 54 (c), Hill Street Studios 42b, Ben Ivory 67/1, Jupiterimages 94br, Ariel Skelley 62/4, Zave Smith 22br, The Image Bank / Shannon Fagan 22bl; **Imagemore Co., Ltd:** 74 (c), 74 (f); **Jupiterimages:** Photos.com 32/1 (a); **Pearson Education Ltd:** Studio 8 104l, Tudor Photography 12/3 & 4; **PhotoDisc:** 24/6, 106/3, Tony Gable. C Squared Studios 74 (e), Photolink 86, StockTrek 87/1 (a), 89/1, 89/2, 89/5; **Shutterstock.com:** Aaron Amat 24/4, Ambient Ideas 26 (g), Atlaspix 60/7, Israel Hervas Bengochea 60/8, ConstantinosZ 74 (j), cowardlion 46br, d13 36/4, Andy Dean Photography 54b, Dja65 106/4, dotshock 62/7, EpicStockMedia 66 (d), First aid 17/5 (first aid box), Gelpi JM 41, Eric Gevaert 32/2 (a), Mandy Godbehear 65l, godrick 87/1 (b), 106/2, Stephen B. Goodwin 26 (b), Janet Faye Hastings 48/4, Mark Herreid 12/1, Tom Hirtreiter 87/3 (a), holbox 47b, Eric Isselee 10 (a), 24/5, jabiru 48/8, JHDT Stock Images LLC 77, Julian W 87/2 (b), Anan Kaewkhammul 32/3 (a), kamilpetran 66 (b), John Kasawa 12/8, Christian Kieffer 66 (c), Kletr 26 (a), Ansis Klucis 74 (g), Tamara Kulikova 17/2, Loo Joo Pheng 27tr, Janelle Lugge 30l, Mazzzur 70 (b), Monkey Business Images 48/9, monticello 17/4 (water), naluwan 10t, Andrey Pavlov 27br, pedalist 38 (c), Richard Peterson 26 (f), Phant 74 (k), photobar 24/2, l. Pilon 36/1, pixbox77 91 (c), pmphoto 87/4 (a), Pyty 70 (a), restyler 17/5 (batteries), rm 32/4 (c), SergiyN 61, somchaij 10 (b), songyos 23 (c), spotmatik 38 (a), Ferenc Szelepcsenyi 36/5, Twonix Studio 103 (c), Beth Van Trees 65r, Francois van Heerden 27tl, Tracy Whiteside 81r; **Sozaijiten:** 74 (a).

Screenshots: Screenshot on page 78 front cover of Diary of a Wimpy Kid by Jeff Kinney (First published in the US by Harry N. Abrams 2007, Puffin Books 2008). Copyright © Jeff Kinney, 2007. Reproduced by permission of Penguin Books Ltd.

All other images © Pearson Education

Every effort has been made to trace the copyright holders and we apologize in advance for any unintentional omissions. We would be pleased to insert the appropriate acknowledgement in any subsequent edition of this publication.

Contents

Scope and sequence 4
Welcome 6
1 Adventure camp 12
Wider World 1 22
2 Wildlife park 24
Review Units 1 and 2 34
3 Where we live 36
Wider World 2 46
4 Good days, bad days 48
Review Units 3 and 4 58
5 Trips 60
Wider World 3 70
6 Arts 72
Review Units 5 and 6 82
7 Space 84
Wider World 4 94
8 The environment 96
Review Units 7 and 8 106
Goodbye 108
Wordlist 112
Verb list 115

Scope and sequence

Welcome

Vocabulary:	**Senses:** look, smell, taste, sound, feel
Structures:	Does it look good? Yes, it does. / No, it doesn't. What does it look like? It looks good. It looks like a cake.

1 Adventure camp

Vocabulary:	**Camping equipment:** sleeping bag, tent, poles, pegs, compass, flashlight, first-aid kit, air mattress, air pump **Camping activities:** pitch the tent, take down the tent, put in the pegs, set up the bed, cover our heads, light a fire, keep out the rain, read a compass	**Cross-curricular:** **Social science:** Being a mountaineer and an adventurer survival kit **Values:** Safety first. Think about safety when you go camping.
Structures:	Flo is good at swimming. I like hiking, but I don't like sailing. I love fishing and camping. I'm pitching the tent. We're putting in the pegs. I can pitch a tent, but I can't read a compass.	

2 Wildlife park

Vocabulary:	**Animals:** rhino, cheetah, panther, meerkat, emu, scorpion, seal, otter, sea turtle, tiger, lemur, koala, whale **Superlative adjectives:** tallest, longest, shortest, biggest, smallest, heaviest, lightest, fastest, slowest	**Cross-curricular:** **Science:** Chameleons kept, in the wild **Values:** Think before you act. Think carefully before making important decisions.
Structures:	How heavy is it? It's 800 kilograms. How tall is it? It's 5 meters tall. The giraffe is taller than the rhino. The giraffe is the tallest. Are otters bigger than seals? Yes, they are. / No, they aren't. Were the giraffes taller than the trees? Yes, they were. / No, they weren't. Which is the heaviest? The hippo is the heaviest.	

3 Where we live

Vocabulary:	**Places:** supermarket, library, park, movie theater, shopping mall, museum, bank, pharmacy, castle hospital, airport, bookstore, station, arcade, coffee shop	**Cross-curricular:** **Geography:** Interesting places **Values:** Learn to be flexible. It can be frustrating when you have to do things you don't want to do. Learn to stay calm and just do it!
Structures:	How do you get to the school? Go straight, then turn left at First Avenue. / It's next to the movie theater. / It's behind the park. / It's at the end of First Avenue. I want to go to the park. / He/She wants to go to the park. I have to go to the library. / He/She has to go to the library.	

4 Good days, bad days

Vocabulary:	**International food dishes:** curry, an omelet, spaghetti, fish and chips, paella, dumplings, sushi, stew, rice and beans, noodles, soup **Verbs and objects:** pack my bag, miss the bus, pass a test, eat my lunch, bring my juice, drop the ball	**Cross-curricular:** **Social science:** Ellen the sailor sailor, alone, broke (the world record) **Values:** Be positive about your day. Don't worry. Be happy.
Structures:	I cooked stew. He dropped the plate. She paddled very quickly. We fell in the lake. What happened? I didn't pass my test because I didn't study. He didn't bring his juice because he was late for school.	

5 Trips

Vocabulary: **Tourist attractions:** aquarium, amusement park, palace, water park, theater, national park, circus, botanical gardens
Amusement park attractions: ride the Ferris wheel, go on the bumper cars, play miniature golf, go on the paddle boats, ride the roller coaster, go on the pirate ship, go on the water slide

Structures: What did you do yesterday? I went to the aquarium.
Did you go to the aquarium? Yes, I did. / No, I didn't.
Did you like the aquarium? Yes, I did. / No, I didn't.
What will you do at the amusement park?
First, I'll ride the Ferris wheel. Then I'll go on the bumper cars.

Cross-curricular:
Social science: Beach safety

Values:
Plan, but be flexible. Planning helps you do more things.

6 Arts

Vocabulary: **Movie genres:** thriller, comedy, sci-fi, romance, musical, cartoon, action, western
Musical instruments: cello, harmonica, saxophone, triangle, drums, clarinet, harp, tambourine, cymbal, maracas, castanets

Structures: I saw the movie by myself.
You wrote it by yourself.
He made it by himself.
She didn't go to the movie by herself.
We didn't watch it by ourselves.
They didn't draw it by themselves.
Did you hear the cello? Yes, I did. / No, I didn't.
Have you ever played the saxophone? Yes, I have. / No, I haven't.
Have you ever been to a concert? Yes, I have. / No, I've never been to a concert.

Cross-curricular:
Literature: Poetry

Values:
Learn to be self-sufficient. You can always do some things by yourself.

7 Space

Vocabulary: **Space:** an astronaut, a planet, a comet, a telescope, an alien, a spaceship, a satellite, the Moon, a star, the Sun
Adjectives: complicated, amazing, frightening, intelligent, brilliant, important, fascinating, gorgeous

Structures: Who are they? They're astronauts.
When did they come? They came last night.
Where did they come from? They came from the Moon.
How did they get here? They came by spaceship.
Why are you looking at the sky? I saw a flashing light.
What's that flashing light? It's a spaceship.
Which telescope is more complicated?
The big telescope is more complicated than the small telescope.
Which telescope is the most complicated?
The big telescope is the most complicated.
Which telescope is less complicated?
The small telescope is less complicated than the big telescope.
Which telescope is the least complicated?
The small telescope is the least complicated.

Cross-curricular:
Science: Space facts
giant leap, mankind, discovery, life, possible

Values:
Use your imagination when you are trying to solve a problem.

8 The environment

Vocabulary: **Ways to help the environment:** recycle paper, recycle bottles, pick up trash, reuse plastic bags, turn off the lights, use public transportation
Environmentally friendly outcomes: recycle paper / save trees, recycle bottles / save resources, pick up trash / keep the planet clean, reuse plastic bags / reduce waste, turn off the lights / conserve energy, use public transportation / reduce pollution

Structures: Are you going to recycle paper? Yes, I am. / No, I'm not. I'm going to recycle bottles.
What can you do to help? I can use public transportation.
If you reuse plastic bags, you'll reduce waste.

Cross-curricular:
Geography: Our amazing world

Values:
Save our planet. Learn to save energy and keep the planet clean.

Welcome

1 🎧 A:02 Talk about the pictures. Then listen and read.

1 IT'S THE YEAR 2084. MATT WORKS AT THE FUTURE ISLAND SCIENCE PARK. IT'S TIME TO GO HOME.

Come on, AL. It's late and I'm tired. Let's go home.

Yes, sir.

2 Hey, AL, does that look strange to you?

Yes, sir. And the time hole detector is buzzing!

BANG

3 WOAH!! OK, that's enough. We're going in!

BANG

4 Hurry up, Dot!

Don't worry! We have all the time in the world with this machine!

5 There's something weird about those guys...

6 OK, I got what we need. We can go now.

Good. I want to go home, Zeb.

Lessons 1 and 2

Can understand a story

7
Shh! What was that?
Quick! We have to leave NOW!
TIME PORT
FLASH
8
Oh, no! They've stolen the new model THD. What should we do?
Our THD has a trace, sir!
9
So where are they now?
In 1950, sir. Something's wrong with the THD. Hold on!
FLASH
10
Um, I don't think this is 1950, AL.
Sorry, sir. The THD is terrible again today! But we still have the trace!
OFFICE
COOKHOUSE
SHOWERS
MUD
11
Oh! Who are you? You look like something out of a sci-fi movie.
Hi, I'm Matt. This is AL.
Our transportation isn't working.
12
THAT's your transportation? It looks like a problem with the CTP port.
Thanks. I'm Bella, by the way.
Wow! You're good.
TO BE CONTINUED...

Matt's office in the Science Park

Travel through time and space with a THD

4 Zeb, Dot

1 Matt
This is Matt. He works at the Science Park on Future Island. He is a time engineer. He works in a very modern office. Matt is hard-working and patient. He often works until late at night.

2 AL
This is AL. He is Matt's droid assistant. He was made with expensive technology. He helps Matt solve difficult problems. They often time-travel together. AL is talkative and very smart. He likes working for Matt.

3 Bella

Lesson 3

Can identify characters in a story

This is the mysterious couple who took the THD. Now they want to go home. They are smart and fast. Who are they? Why did they take the technology? Matt wants to know the answers to these questions.

This is Bella. Bella is at an adventure camp. She joins Matt and AL on their mission. She will try to help them find the mysterious couple. Bella is smart, creative, and helpful. She is good at computers and is never bored.

2 Work with a friend and write. What things can you see in Future Island that we do not have now?

1 _____
2 _____
3 _____
4 _____

3 A:03 Listen and read about Matt, AL, and Bella. Then write.

1 What's Matt's job?
He _____.
2 What's AL's job?
He _____.
3 Where is Bella?
She _____.
4 What do the mysterious couple want to do?
They _____.

4 Correct the sentences.

1 Matt doesn't work at the Science Park.
_____

2 Bella doesn't understand computers.
_____

3 AL isn't talkative.
_____

4 The mysterious couple are slow and stupid.
_____

5 Ask and answer. What do you think will happen in the story?

I think Matt will…

I think the mysterious couple will…

I think Bella will…

Lesson 4

Can describe characters in a story

6 Listen and say.

LOOK!

Does it look good?	Yes, it does. / No, it doesn't.
What does it look like?	It looks good.
	It looks like a cake.

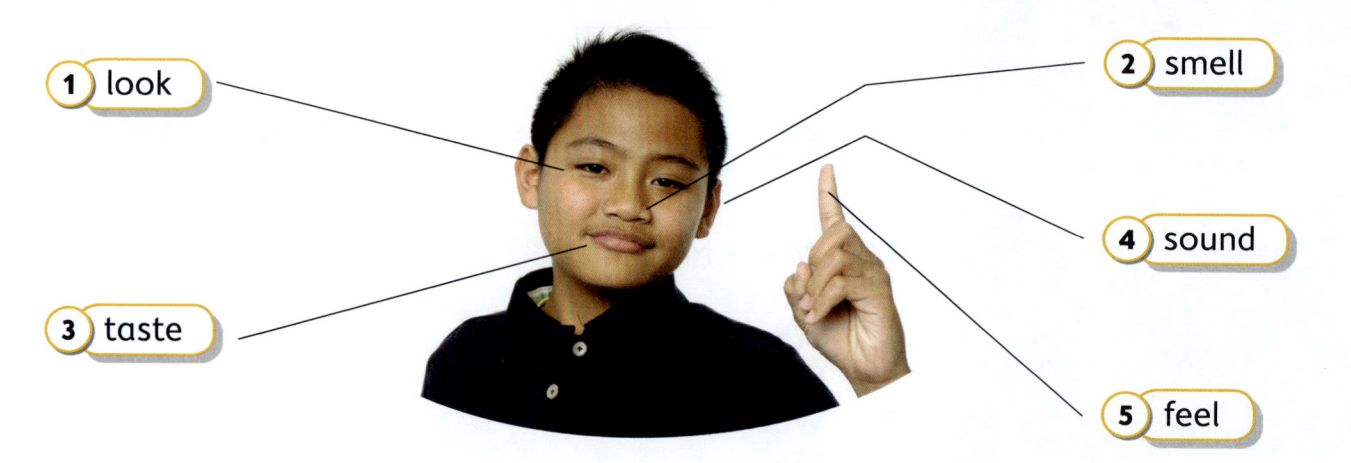

1. look
2. smell
3. taste
4. sound
5. feel

7 Listen and check (✓). Then number the pictures.

	looks		feels		smells/sounds/tastes	
1	scary ☐	hard ☐	spiky ☐	soft ☐	nice ☐	sweet ☐
2	round ☐	red ☐	smooth ☐	hard ☐	loud ☐	quiet ☐
3	cute ☐	scary ☐	hot ☐	furry ☐		
4	wild ☐	wet ☐	cold ☐	hot ☐		

a b c d

8 Look at Activity 7 and write.

1 The _____ feels _____ and tastes _____.
2 The _____ looks _____ and _____ loud.
3 The _____.
4 The ice cube _____.

Lesson 5

Can recognize what something looks/smells/tastes/sounds/feels like

9 Ask and answer.

What does it look like?

It looks like a river.

It's Picture 1.

That's right!

10 Play the guessing game.

How to play

Your friend looks at Number 1 and thinks of a fruit. Ask questions: "Does it taste sweet?" "Does it feel spiky?" Check (✓) the question box each time you ask a question. How many questions did it take to get the correct fruit? Play again with Number 2.

Check (✓) a box each time you ask a question. How many questions did you ask?

	Question 1	Question 2	Question 3	Question 4	Question 5	Question 6	Question 7	Question 8
1 fruit								
2 vegetable								
3 clothes								
4 drink								
5 animal								

Lesson 6 — Can ask and answer about what something looks/smells/tastes/sounds/feels like

1 Adventure camp

1 ⭐ What camping words do you know? Can you say them?

2 🎧 A:07 Listen and read. What things do they have?

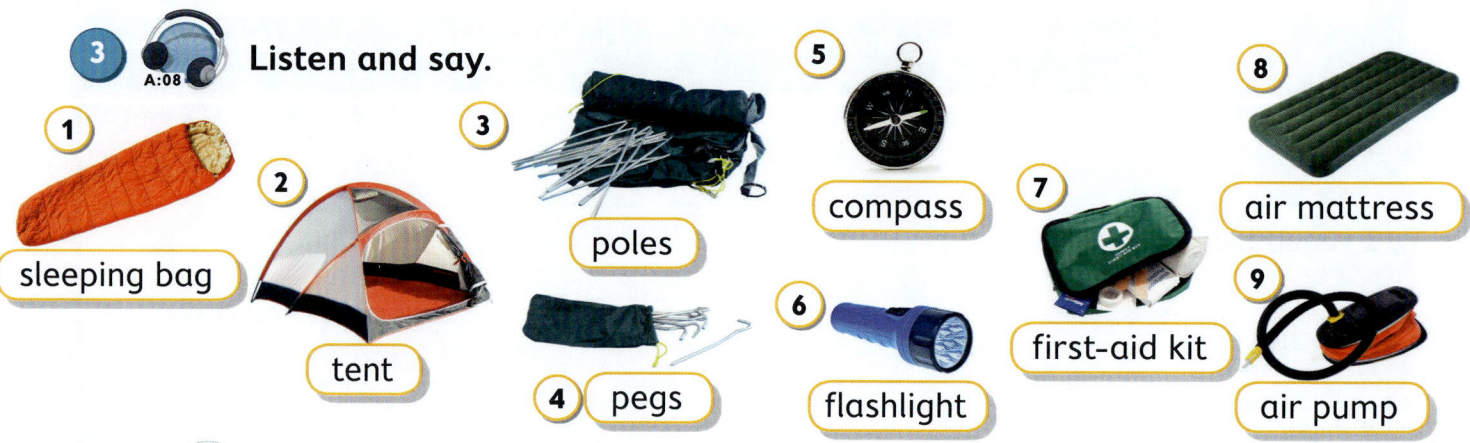

1 Hi, I'm Hannah. Welcome to this summer's adventure camp.

2 OK. I can see your sleeping bags, but who has the tent, poles, and pegs?

I have the tent, Felipe has the poles, and Maria has the pegs.

I have a big flashlight and four compasses.

3 OK. Let's pitch the tent and make a campfire.

Great!

4 This is the week's schedule. There's lots to do!

3 🎧 A:08 Listen and say.

1. sleeping bag
2. tent
3. poles
4. pegs
5. compass
6. flashlight
7. first-aid kit
8. air mattress
9. air pump

4 Play the memory game.

A: I went camping, and in my tent there was a sleeping bag.
B: I went camping, and in my tent there was a sleeping bag and a...

12 Lesson 1   Can identify camping equipment

5 Listen and read. Then circle T = True or F = False.

LOOK!

Flo is good at swimming.
I like hiking, but **I don't like** sailing.
I love fishing and camping.

a My name's Tom. I'm 14, and I'm American. I love playing basketball and soccer. I can cook and swim, but I can't surf. I have one sister, Flo. She's 12, and she's very funny.

b My name's Maria, and I'm 13. I'm from Mexico. I like dancing, but I'm not very good at singing! I have two sisters. They're 8 and 10, and I love playing with them!

c I'm Flo, and I'm 12. I'm from the United States. I'm good at swimming. I love talking to my friends. I have one brother. He's 14, and he's very good at sports.

d I'm Felipe. I'm from Spain. I'm 13. I love playing video games, and I like science and math. I have three brothers, and they love video games, too. We always have competitions!

1 Tom can swim and surf. T / F
2 Maria is Mexican. T / F
3 Flo is good at swimming. T / F
4 Flo loves talking to her friends. T / F
5 Felipe only has two brothers. T / F

6 Ask and answer.

1 Where are Tom and Flo from?
2 What does Tom love doing?
3 How old are Maria's sisters?
4 What subjects does Felipe like?

7 Imagine you are Tom, Maria, Flo, or Felipe. Ask and answer.

1 How old are you?
2 Where are you from?
3 What do you like doing?
4 What are you good at?
5 Do you have any brothers or sisters?

Lesson 2

Can talk about what people *like/don't like/are good at* doing

8 Listen and number. Then say.

a pitch the tent
b take down the tent
c put in the pegs
d set up the bed
e cover our heads
f light a fire
g keep out the rain
h read a compass

VOCABULARY

9 Listen to the song and write.

SONG

Scouts around the world, from Spain to Mexico.
We're traveling together, from the mountains to the ocean.
We're walking for miles and learning every day.
We're reading a ¹_____ and finding our way.

Chorus:
Oh, we are adventure campers, here is our song.
With adventure and new friends, you can't go wrong!
At the end of the day, we're back to camp again.
We're pitching our ²_____, they keep out the rain.
We're putting in the ³_____ and setting up our ⁴_____.
We're sleeping in ⁵_____ that cover our heads!
(Chorus)
All this adventure is making us fit and strong.
We're cooking our food, which doesn't take too long.
We're eating our dinner, and then we're so tired.
We're sleeping in tents all around the ⁶_____!
(Chorus)

10 Look at Activity 9 and check (✓) the activities in the song.

1 reading a compass
2 wearing sunglasses
3 pitching tents
4 putting in the pegs
5 running a race
6 taking down the tent

Lesson 3

Can identify camping activities

11 Listen and number the pictures. Then match.

a   Today is the last day, so we're taking down the tent.

b   I'm at the campsite, and I'm pitching the tent.

c   I'm lost, so I'm reading a compass.

d   I'm putting in the pegs.

e   I want to cook dinner, so I'm lighting a fire.

f   It's raining, so we're covering our heads.

g   It's evening now, so I'm setting up the bed.

LOOK!

I'm pitching the tent.

We're putting in the pegs.

I can pitch a tent, but I can't read a compass.

12 Listen and match. Then say.

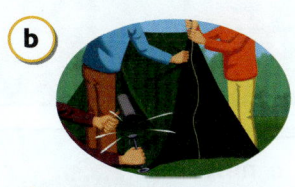

13 What can you do? Ask and answer.

She can light a fire, but she can't read a compass.

Lesson 4   Can talk about what I'm doing and what someone can and can't do

15

14 🎧 A:17 Talk about the pictures. Then listen and read. **STORY**

MATT IS TELLING BELLA ABOUT THEIR TIME JOURNEY.

1
... so these weird guys took our new THD and went off in time!
There! Your – thingy – is working now. What is it anyway?

2
It's a THD, a time hole detector. It's what the thieves took. You can travel through time with it.
Wow! Can we try it?

3
Don't you have stuff to do here?
Um, not really.

TODAY'S TASKS
PITCH TENTS
READ COMPASSES
LIGHT FIRES
KEEP OUT OF THE RAIN
TAKE DOWN TENTS

4
This looks fun! Don't you like camping?
Yes, I love camping, but come on, TIME TRAVEL!!?

5
Sir! There's a new trace! They're going to – Africa!
Oh, WOW! Please let me come.
She is good at computers, sir. That could be useful.

6
You can bring me back in time. Oh, PLEASE!!!
Oh, all right.
AL, let's follow those guys.

15 What is a THD? What can you do with it? Discuss your answers.

Lesson 5 — Can understand a simple story / Can discuss a story

16 **Circle the correct answer.**

1. The THD is (working / not working) now.
2. Bella (likes / doesn't like) camping.
3. Bella (doesn't have / has) a lot of tasks to do today.
4. AL (doesn't want / wants) Bella to come with them.
5. The mysterious couple is (going to / not going to) Africa.

17 **Complete the summary.**

> Africa   Bella   camp   computers   THD   time-travel

Matt and AL use the ¹_____ to follow the mysterious couple. They arrive at an adventure ²_____, and they meet ³_____. She's good at ⁴_____, and she wants to ⁵_____ with Matt and AL. Matt says all right. They follow the mysterious couple to ⁶_____.

18 **Role-play the story.**

19 **Number to match the instructions to the headings.**

- [ ] Food and water
- [ ] Things you need
- [ ] Making a fire
- [ ] Pitching the tent
- [ ] Choosing the right spot

VALUES
Safety first. Think about safety when you go camping.

1. Always choose a flat, high spot to set up camp – not near a river or mountain slope.

2. Clean the ground and pitch the tent. The door should face the rising sun.

3. The fire shouldn't be too close to the tents or under tree branches.

4. Take a lot of drinking water, dry foods (pasta, noodles, rice, cookies, nuts, and raisins), and canned foods (soups and vegetables).

5. Take insect repellent, sunblock, a first-aid kit, a flashlight, matches, batteries, and a gas stove.

HOME SCHOOL LINK Tell your family why camping safety is important.

Lesson 6 — Can understand details of a story / Can recognize why camping safety is important

20 Listen and read the letter. Where was Flo yesterday? Then write the words.

> campfire   dinner   friends   Spain   Spanish   wildlife

Dear Mom,

How are you? It's our second day at adventure camp, and we're having a great time. We have some new friends, too – they're from ¹_____ and Mexico. They're teaching me ²_____, but I'm not very good at it!

Our first night was great. There was a big ³_____ to welcome everyone, and there were songs by the ⁴_____. After the campfire, we went to bed. At night, our tent was cold, but it was warm in the sleeping bag.

Today, we're walking to a ⁵_____ park that's next to the camp.

Here's a photo of me with my new ⁶_____ and a photo of last night's campfire.

Love to you and Dad,

Flo

21 Answer the questions.

1. Where are Flo's new friends from?
   They're from _____.
2. What is Flo learning?
   She's _____.
3. What did they do to welcome everybody?
   There _____.
4. Where are they going today?
   _____

22 Ask and answer.

1. Do you like camping?
2. Where do you go camping?
3. What activities do you do there?

Lesson 7

Can understand a letter about being on adventure camp

SOCIAL SCIENCE 1

23 ⭐ What do you know?

24 🎧 A:19 Listen and read. What is Bear's job?

Bear Grylls

Bear Grylls is a mountaineer and adventurer. He went up Mount Everest when he was just 23 years old! Bear usually lives in the United Kingdom, but sometimes he lives in the desert, the mountains, or the jungle. He is also Chief Scout of Scouts UK.

1 What do you like doing?
I like playing the guitar, running, doing yoga, and playing with my children.

2 Do you like living in the jungle?
I love jungles, but they're difficult to live in. There are often a lot of snakes and insects.
Sometimes I sleep up in a tree and when it rains, it's horrible.

3 Where is your favorite place?
An island in Indonesia. I love visiting islands, and this one was really beautiful.

4 What do you do before an adventure?
I always learn a lot about where I want to go – I learn about the plants and animals.
I train six days a week, and I run and do yoga, too. I also prepare my survival kit.

5 Are you scared of anything?
Yes, I'm scared of high buildings and mountains. I can go to the top of high buildings, but I don't like it.

25 Circle T = True or F = False.

1 Bear does yoga before a trip. T / F
2 Jungles are difficult to live in. T / F
3 Bear doesn't take a survival kit. T / F

I'm going to Mount Everest in Nepal.

I'm going to take a big backpack with a lot of things...

MINI PROJECT

26 Prepare for an adventure trip.

- **Ideas** – Imagine you are going to the jungle or mountains.
- **Plan** – Make notes. Where you are going? What do you need to take?
- **Write** – Answer these questions with 1–2 sentences. Where are you going? Why? How can you prepare? What will you take? What are you scared of?
- **Share** – Interview a classmate about their adventure.

Lesson 8 — Can understand a text about an adventurer / Can plan an adventure trip

27 Match.

1. You do this to find your way.
2. You put these in when pitching the tent.
3. You do this before going to sleep.
4. You do this before you go home.
5. You are warm when you use this.

a. sleeping bag
b. read a compass
c. pegs
d. set up the bed
e. take down the tent

I CAN DO IT!

28 Listen and ✓ or ✗.

		likes	loves	is good at
1	Sally	a	b	c
2	Pete	a	b	c

29 Unscramble and write questions. Then look at Activity 28 and write answers.

1. Sally / doing / love / does / what
   _____
2. Sally / what / at / good / is
   _____
3. Pete / a / is / compass / at / reading / good
   _____

30 Ask and answer.

1. What do you like doing? What do you not like doing?
2. What are you good at? What are you not good at?
3. What do you do when you go camping?

I CAN

I can identify camping equipment and activities.
I can talk about what people *like/don't like/are good at* doing.
I can plan an adventure trip.

Lesson 9

Can assess what I have learned in Unit 1

HAVE FUN 1

What are you good at?

31 Write answers about you. Then guess about your partner.

What are you good at?
1 _____ 2 _____
What are you not good at?
1 _____ 2 _____
What do you like doing?
1 _____ 2 _____
What don't you like doing?
1 _____ 2 _____
What subjects do you like?
1 _____ 2 _____
What subjects don't you like?
1 _____ 2 _____
What sports do you like?
1 _____ 2 _____
What sports don't you like?
1 _____ 2 _____

32 ⭐ What did you enjoy in this unit? What do you want to know more about?

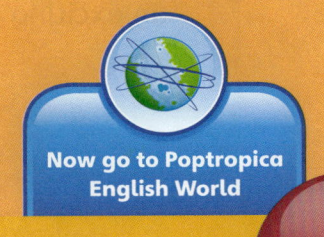

Now go to Poptropica English World

Lesson 10   Can use what I have learned in Unit 1   21

Wider World 1
Camping around the world

1 What do you know?

2 Look at pictures a–c and make sentences.

> There's a cave. There are some trees.

3 Listen and read. Then number the pictures in Activity 2.

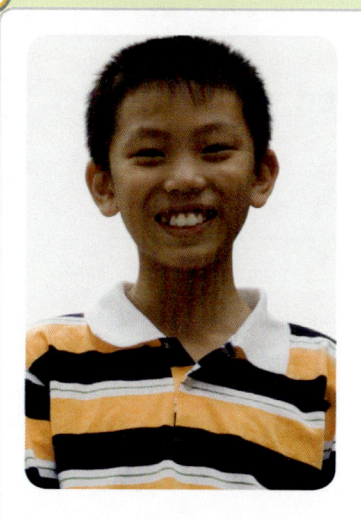

1
Camping in Thailand is a lot of fun. My favorite place is a National Park called Khao Sam Roi Yot. Khao Sam Roi Yot means the mountain with 300 peaks. The mountains are very difficult to climb. There are a lot of things to see around the park. I like watching the beautiful birds and other wild animals like deer and squirrels. There are a lot of interesting caves, too. Thailand is an exciting place!

Alak, 12, Thailand

2
Death Valley National Park in California is a great place for desert camping. It's very hot there in the summer. I usually visit Death Valley in the spring with my family. I love riding my bike on the paths in the mountains. Mountain biking is difficult, but it's very exciting. My dad likes making big campfires in the evening. He likes cooking our dinner on the fire. There are many types of snakes, lizards, and birds in Death Valley. It's never boring in the desert!

Melissa, 12, United States

Wider World 1 — Can understand texts about camping around the world

3

Vulcano is a small volcanic island in Italy. I like camping there in the summer with my grandparents. We sleep in a small cabin in the forest. During the day, my grandpa rides a motorbike around the island. I like hiking to the top of the volcano. My grandma likes walking on the black sandy beaches near the sea. There is special mud in Vulcano that is very good for your skin. Some people like putting the mud on their bodies. I love visiting Vulcano!

Luca, 11, Italy

4 Circle T = True or F = False.

1 The mountains of Thailand are easy to climb. T / F
2 Alak likes watching birds. T / F
3 Death Valley is in the desert. T / F
4 Melissa doesn't like riding her bike. T / F
5 Vulcano is a big island. T / F
6 Luca likes hiking. T / F

5 Ask and answer.

1 Do you like camping?
2 Where can you camp in your country?

YOUR TURN!

Describe an ideal camping trip. Think about these things.

What's the place's name? Where is it?
What's the place like?
What can you do there?
What should you take with you?
Why is it ideal for you?

Can talk about camping in my country

2 Wildlife park

1 ⭐ Do you know the names of any wild animals? What can you say about them?

2 🎧 A:22 Listen and read. Where was Flo?

1. What did you learn today?
2. We were with the cheetahs. They were really fast! Cheetahs are the fastest animals on Earth.
3. I was with the snakes. They were really long. One of them is the longest type of snake in the world!
4. I was with the elephant. Cool! How big was it? Really big, and heavy – it's 3,000 kilograms!

3 🎧 A:23 Listen and say.

1. rhino
2. cheetah
3. panther
4. meerkat
5. emu
6. scorpion
7. seal
8. otter
9. sea turtle
10. tiger
11. lemur
12. koala
13. whale

4 Play the game. How many animals can you guess?

A: Long and thin! **B:** Snakes!

Lesson 1

Can identify wild animals

5 Look and listen. Which animal is Tom describing?

LOOK!

How heavy is it?	It's 800 kilograms.
How tall is it?	It's 5 meters tall.

The giraffe **is taller than** the rhino.
The giraffe **is the tallest**.

Name: Roddy
How heavy? 1,600 kilograms
How tall? 2 meters
How long? 3 meters
How fast? fast!

Name: Geri
How heavy? 800 kilograms
How tall? 5 meters
How long? 3 meters
How fast? fast!

6 Look and ask questions.

1. tall / the giraffe?
2. heavy / the rhino?
3. fast / the rhino?
4. long / the giraffe?
5. tall / the rhino?
6. heavy / the giraffe?

How tall is the giraffe?
It's 5 meters tall.

7 Look. Then ask and answer. What animal is it?

How tall is it?
It's 3.5 meters tall.

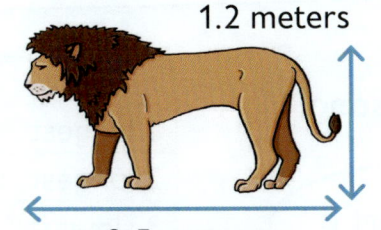

0.8 meters
1.8 meters
50 kilograms

1.2 meters
2.5 meters
200 kilograms

3.5 meters
7 meters
5,000 kilograms

Lesson 2

Can ask and answer about animals using *How tall/heavy/long/fast is it?*

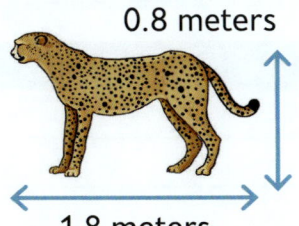

25

8 Listen and number. Then say.

VOCABULARY

a tallest
b longest
c shortest
d biggest
e smallest
f heaviest
g lightest
h fastest
i slowest

9 Listen to the song and write.

SONG

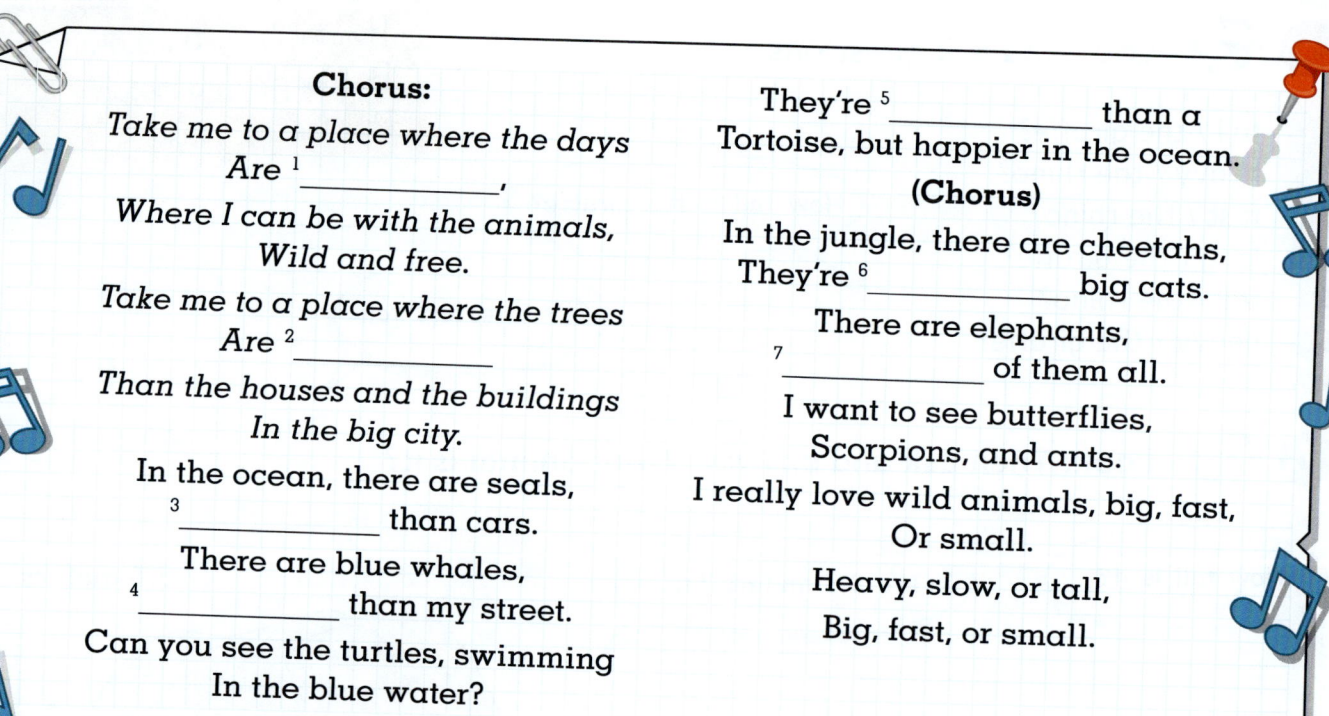

Chorus:
Take me to a place where the days
Are ¹_____,
Where I can be with the animals,
Wild and free.
Take me to a place where the trees
Are ²_____
Than the houses and the buildings
In the big city.
In the ocean, there are seals,
³_____ than cars.
There are blue whales,
⁴_____ than my street.
Can you see the turtles, swimming
In the blue water?

They're ⁵_____ than a
Tortoise, but happier in the ocean.
(Chorus)
In the jungle, there are cheetahs,
They're ⁶_____ big cats.
There are elephants,
⁷_____ of them all.
I want to see butterflies,
Scorpions, and ants.
I really love wild animals, big, fast,
Or small.
Heavy, slow, or tall,
Big, fast, or small.

10 Ask and answer about the song.

Which animal in the song is the biggest?

The elephant is the biggest.

	Animal
1 biggest	
2 longest	
3 slowest	
4 fastest	

Lesson 3

Can talk about which animal is *the biggest/longest/slowest/fastest*

SKILLS 2

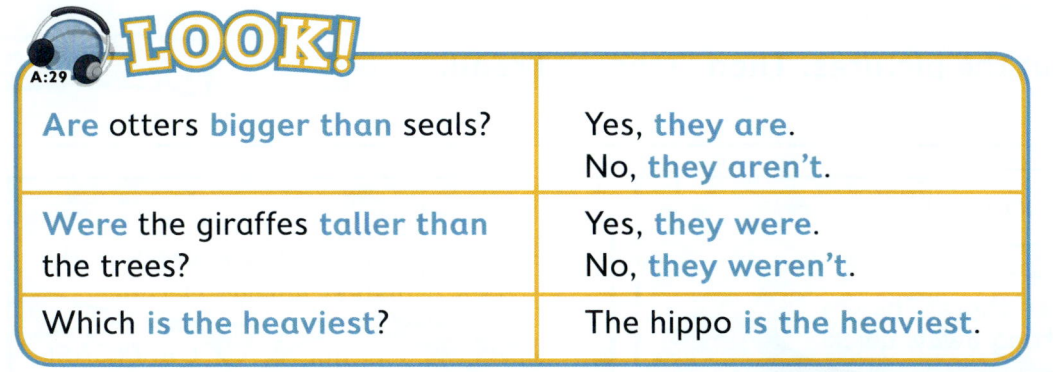

LOOK!

Are otters bigger than seals?	Yes, they are. / No, they aren't.
Were the giraffes taller than the trees?	Yes, they were. / No, they weren't.
Which is the heaviest?	The hippo is the heaviest.

11 Listen. Then ask and answer.

1. Are rhinos heavier than seals?
   _____
2. Which animal is the fastest?
   _____
3. Are snakes louder than lemurs?
   _____
4. Which animal is the shortest?
   _____

Which animal is the tallest? Are tigers taller than otters?

Giraffes are the tallest. Tigers are taller than otters.

12 Read and say.

1. giraffes / otters / tigers (tall)
2. koalas / lemurs / turtles (slow)
3. elephants / turtles / hippos (heavy)
4. panthers / giraffes / cheetahs (fast)

13 Look at the table. Ask and answer.

Which animal...?

Life Span

Animal	In the zoo	In the wild
rhino	35 years	30 years
lemur	27 years	15 years
panda	20 years	10 years

1. Which animal has the longest life?
2. Which animal has the shortest life?
3. Where do these animals live a longer life? Why?
4. Where do these animals live a shorter life? Why?

Lesson 4 — Can compare animals using *bigger/longer/slower/faster than*

14 Talk about the pictures. Then listen and read. **STORY**

1 THE THD IS WORKING NOW.
- I can't see anyone.
- Over there! They're getting away, quick!

2
- Rhinos can run at 50 km per hour. But the cheetah is the fastest animal. It can…
- Oh, um, quick!
- Oh, PLEASE be QUIET!

3
- Is the rhino still there?
- No. And those guys that took the THD aren't here either.
- Um, how do we get down?

4
- It's lucky I had this rope.
- Yeah, and you can tie knots!

5
- Um, is that a cheetah?
- The cheetah is the fastest animal…
- Hello, little guy.

6
- QUICK! Get us out of here!

15 How do Matt and Bella get away from the rhino? What does Bella do?

Lesson 5 — Can understand a simple story / Can discuss a story

16 Circle the correct answer.

1 Why is Matt angry with AL?
   a He talks too much.   b He runs too slowly.   c He climbs too fast.
2 What animal does Bella say hello to?
   a the rhino   b the meerkat   c the cheetah
3 How do they get away from the cheetah?
   a They climb a tree.   b They run very fast.   c They use the THD.

17 Complete the summary.

> Africa   cheetah   couple   rhino   rope   THD

Matt, Bella, and AL arrive in ¹_____. They want to talk to the mysterious ²_____. Matt sees them, but he also sees a ³_____. Matt, Bella, and AL all run fast to get away. They use Bella's ⁴_____ to climb a tree. They get down from the tree, but then they see that a ⁵_____ is coming! They use the ⁶_____ to get away quickly.

18 Role-play the story.

VALUES
Think before you act. Think carefully before making important decisions.

19 Read the situations. Check (✓) the best thing to do.

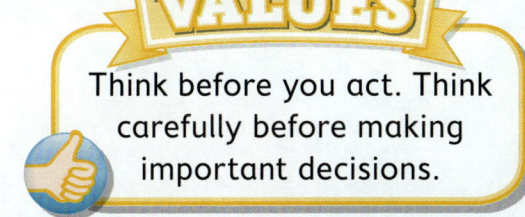

	1	2	3
A Tomorrow is the deadline for entering a story-writing competition. What do you do?	You're not happy with your writing, but you sign up immediately.	You're not happy with your writing. You ask your teacher for advice and then decide.	You don't enter the competition because you're not happy with your writing.
B Your best friend is not talking to you. He/She looks angry, but you don't know why. What do you do?	You text your friend and invite him/her to meet you after school.	You leave a note on your friend's desk to ask what's wrong.	You find your friend at school and ask what's wrong.

HOME SCHOOL LINK Tell your family about an important decision you made today.

Lesson 6 — Can understand details of a story / Can recognize the importance of thinking before you act

20 Listen and read. Is Vernie happier now?

PLEASE SPONSOR VERNIE!

HOME | ABOUT US | CONTACT US

Please sponsor me!

VERNIE'S STORY

Here at the reserve, we have a lot of rescued koalas. They live longer here, and they are happier here than in the wild.

Vernie the koala was in the wild for years. Her home was next to a road. It was very dangerous. Then one day, the saddest thing happened to her. Her joey, a baby koala, died on the road. Vernie was very unhappy.

We went to the forest one day, looking for sick koalas. Vernie was next to the road. She was not happy, and she was sick.

Now, she is safe and healthy in our koala reserve. She's the happiest koala here. Please sponsor her!

To sponsor Vernie now, click on this link.

21 Write the answers.

1. Where was Vernie's home? _____
2. What does "joey" mean? _____
3. What was the saddest thing to happen to Vernie? _____
4. Was Vernie healthy in the wild? _____
5. Where is Vernie now? _____
6. Is Vernie happier now? _____

22 Look at the words. Compare koalas with other animals.

heavier   lighter   shorter   slower   smaller

Lesson 7

Can understand a text about a rescued koala

SCIENCE 2

23 What do you know?

24 Find the chameleons in the pictures. Then listen and read.

Cool camouflage for chameleons!

Chameleons are one of the strangest animals in the world. There are 160 kinds of chameleons, and many can change color. Here are some more facts about them.

Size: They are sometimes smaller than your finger. Some are longer than your arm! Females are often smaller than males.

Body: They have very long tongues, and their feet have claws. They are very good at climbing.

Color: Chameleons are very smart – they use color to show how they feel or to hide. They can change color when they are scared, angry, hot, or cold. For example, a panther chameleon turns red when it is angry.

Places: A lot of chameleons live in Madagascar in Africa. Some live in India, too. They like hot, dry places.

Food: Chameleons eat insects, and they are good at catching flies with their long tongues. Some big chameleons can eat small birds.

Life Span: They usually live for five to ten years. They live longer when they are kept as pets than in the wild.

25 Ask and answer.

1. What do chameleons look like?
2. When do they change color?
3. Where do they live?
4. What do they eat?

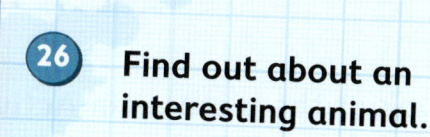

MINI PROJECT

26 Find out about an interesting animal.

- **Ideas** – Think about the most interesting animal you know.
- **Plan** – Make notes about size/body/color/places/food/lifespan.
- **Write** – Write 1–2 sentences about each of these things.
- **Share** – Tell a classmate about your animal.

Lesson 8 Can understand a text about a chameleon / Can find out and write about an interesting animal

27 Read and circle.

1. The giraffe is 5 (kilograms / **meters**) tall.
2. How (**heavy** / tall / long) is the rhino? It's 1,600 kilograms.
3. Cheetahs are the (fast / faster / **fastest**) animal.
4. Meerkats are (**smaller** / bigger / smallest / biggest) than lemurs.

28 Listen, check (✓), and circle.

1. a   b
   bigger / faster

2. a   b
   lighter / taller

3. a   b   c
   fastest / faster

4. a   b   c
   fastest / heaviest

29 Look at Activity 28 and write.

1. The panther is bigger than the cheetah.
2. _____
3. _____
4. _____

30 Look at the pictures in Activity 28. Ask and answer about the animals.

A: Are otters bigger than turtles?
The otter is the lightest.

B: No, they aren't.
Which animal is the lightest?

I CAN

I can talk about which animal is *the biggest/longest/slowest/fastest*.
I can compare animals using *bigger/longer/slower/faster than*.
I can find out and write about an interesting animal.

32 Lesson 9   Can assess what I have learned in Unit 2

31 Read the clues. Write the animals' names.

HAVE FUN 2

Down

1 It's the second largest of all land animals and has one or two horns.
2 It looks like a small monkey and has a long tail.
4 It's the largest land animal.
5 It's an orange cat with black stripes.
9 It's an African animal that has black and white stripes.
10 It's a large animal with flippers. It eats fish and lives in and near the ocean.
13 This animal is the "king" of the animal world.

Across

3 It's the fastest land animal in the world.
6 It's a very large mammal that lives in the ocean.
7 This animal eats fish and is about 1 meter long.
8 It's in the cat family and is usually black.
11 It's a large ocean reptile that has a thick shell.
12 It's quieter than a chimpanzee but much bigger.
14 It's an Australian animal that looks like a small bear.

32 Look at Unit 1, page 12. Ask and answer more questions with –er and –est words.

> Is the first-aid kit lighter than the compass?

> Is the tent the heaviest thing we need for camping?

33 What did you enjoy in this unit? What do you want to know more about?

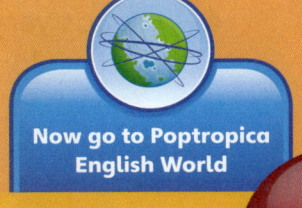

Now go to Poptropica English World

Lesson 10

Review Units 1 and 2

1 Unscramble and write the camping words.

1. plesengi gba
2. slope
3. etnt
4. spge
5. ihtglfhsal
6. mosacsp

2 Read and number the pictures.

1 I'm putting in the pegs.
2 He's setting up the bed.
3 The tent is keeping out the rain.
4 She's covering her head.
5 We're pitching a tent.

a   b    c    d    e

3 Read and circle.

Hello, I'm Hannah. I'm studying to be a vet. I don't like working in offices, but I love working with animals. I like camping, too. I'm good at climbing and pitching tents. I'm working as a youth leader at an adventure camp. Last summer, I went to Uganda, in Africa. We went to the jungle and also on a safari tour. It was very hot in Africa, but there were a lot of interesting animals. The heaviest animal I saw was a rhino. It was more than 1,500 kilograms. That's heavier than my car.

1 Hannah is studying to be a…
   a cook.   b vet.   c youth leader.
2 She's good at…
   a climbing.   b jumping on the trampoline.   c diving.
3 Last summer, Hannah went to…
   a Argentina.   b Uganda.   c Brazil.
4 It was very… in Africa.
   a cold.   b hot.   c rainy.
5 The rhino was the… animal she saw in Africa.
   a biggest   b heaviest   c fastest

4 Ask and answer.

Picture A

Picture B

A: The giraffe is taller than the rhino.
B: It's Picture A.

A: The snake is the longest.
B: It's Picture B.

A: Which koala is the biggest?
B: The koala in Picture A is the biggest.

A: Which animal is the heaviest?
B: I think the seal in Picture A is the heaviest.

5 Guess the animal. Write.

cheetah   elephant   giraffe   panther   whale

1 It likes eating leaves. It's the tallest animal in the world.   _____
2 It's heavier than a cheetah but lighter than a tiger.   _____
3 It's the biggest, heaviest animal in the ocean.   _____
4 It is taller than a rhino but shorter than a giraffe.   _____
5 It's the fastest land animal in the world.   _____

3 Where we live

1 ⭐ What names of places in a town do you know? Can you say them?

2 🎧 A:35 Listen and read. What is Flo doing?

1
- Phew! 450 steps!
- I'm hot now! I want to go swimming! Where's the swimming pool?
- It's there – near the movie theater.
- Then we can go to the park, there, opposite the school. But where's Flo?

2
- Look! She's there – near the park. What's she doing?
- She's buying ice cream! I want ice cream, too! Come on!

3 🎧 A:36 Listen and say.

1. supermarket
2. library
3. park
4. movie theater
5. shopping mall
6. museum
7. bank
8. pharmacy
9. castle

4 🎧 A:37 Look at Activity 2. Listen and number.

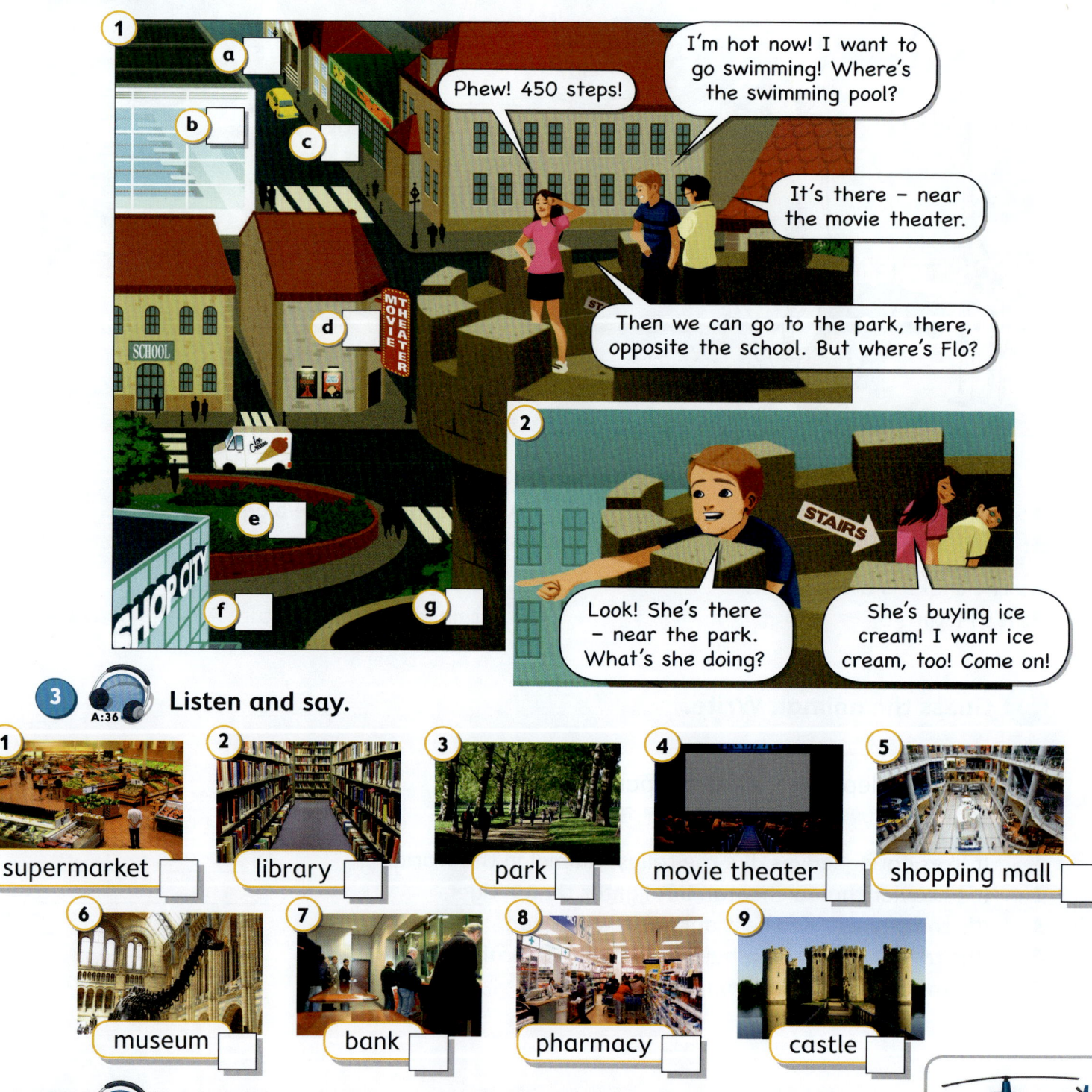

36 Lesson 1

Can identify places in a town

5 Listen and check (✓). Then say.

The van is in front of the supermarket.

LOOK!

How **do you get** to the school?
Go straight, then **turn** left at First Avenue.
It's **next to** the movie theater.
It's **behind** the park.
It's **at the end of** First Avenue.

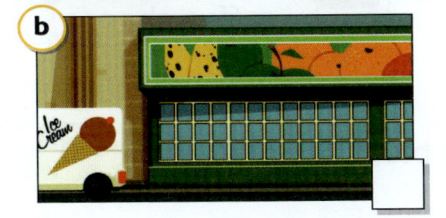

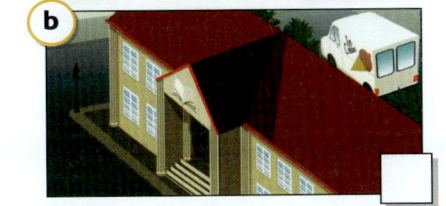

6 Ask and answer.

at the corner   at the end of   behind   go straight   next to   turn left/turn right

1   How do you get to the school?
2   How do you get to the pharmacy?
3   How do you get from the pharmacy to the supermarket?

Could you repeat that?

Let me check… Is it…?

TIP!
It's good to check directions to make sure you understand them.

Lesson 2   Can say where places are and give directions

7 Listen and number. Then say.

a hospital
b airport
c bookstore
d station
e arcade
f coffee shop

8 Listen and clap when you hear the words in blue. Then sing.

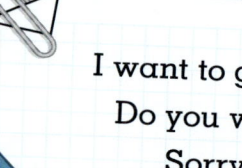

I want to go to the shopping mall.
Do you want to come with me?
Sorry, I can't, my friend.
I want to go to the shopping mall,
But I have to do other things.
Chorus:
There are many things I want to do.
But I can't, my friend. I can't today.
I have to go to the bookstore.
I have to go to the library.
I have to go to the airport,
To pick up a friend.

I want to go to the movie theater.
Do you want to come with me?
Sorry, I can't, my friend.
I want to go to the movie theater,
But I have to do other things.
(Chorus)
I want to go to the park.
Do you want to come with me?
Sorry, I can't, my friend.
I want to go to the park,
But I have to do other things.
(Chorus)

9 Read the song and write.

Where does the girl want to go?
1 She wants to _____.
2 _____
3 _____

Where does the boy have to go?
1 He has to _____.
2 _____
3 _____

Lesson 3

LOOK!

I **want to go** to the park.
I **have to go** to the library.

He/She **wants to go** to the park.
He/She **has to go** to the library.

10 Listen and circle. Then match and say.

1 want to / have to — a (LIBRARY)
2 want to / have to — b (SUPERMARKET)
3 want to / have to — c (DENTIST)
4 want to / have to — d (AIRPORT)
5 want to / have to — e (HOSPITAL)
6 want to / have to — f (BANK)

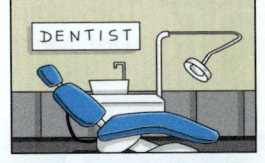

11 Look at Activity 10 and write.

1 She has to go to the dentist.
2 _____
3 _____
4 _____
5 _____
6 _____

Lesson 4 Can use the phrases *want to go* and *have to go* somewhere

12 🎧 A:45   Talk about the pictures. Then listen and read.   **STORY**

1 IN THE LOST WORLD OF ATLANTIS
ATLANTIS
We're in Atlantis?
Yes, those weird guys that took the THD were here. Come on, let's go to the control center.

2 What are those guys doing?
I think they're looking for something.
MALL OCEAN CONTROL CENTER

3 They were here. They said their names are Zeb and Dot Martin. They wanted to buy a space-time chip, model 3PX40.
A what?

4 It's an important chip for a time-travel machine.
There are three in the THD. And I have a spare 3PX40 in here.
Guys, someone's coming! Quick, hide!

5 Where are we going now?
Well, I'm hungry.
MALL

6 And I think Zeb and Dot Martin are hungry, too.

13 Why do you think Dot and Zeb Martin want the space-time chip? Discuss your answers.

Lesson 5

14 Write the missing words. Then number the story events in order.

> are looking for   arrive   hide   hungry   Martin   see

☐ In the control center, they _____ a video of the people that took the THD.
☐ A security guard comes, and they have to _____.
☐ Matt says he is _____, and they leave.
☐ The Martins _____ a space-time chip.
☐ Matt, Bella, and AL _____ in Atlantis.
☐ AL says their names are Zeb and Dot _____.

15 Correct the mistakes.

1 Dot and Zeb Martin want to buy a THD.
   _____

2 The mysterious couple are Bella and Matt.
   _____

3 The 3PX40 isn't important for a time-travel machine.
   _____

VALUES

Learn to be flexible. It can be frustrating when you have to do things you don't want to do. Learn to stay calm and just do it!

16 Role-play the story.

17 How flexible are you? Rank 1 to 5. Then share with a friend.

SITUATION	A You want to play video games, but you have to do homework.	B You want to go to a party, but you have to be home before 10 p.m.	C You want to meet your friends, but you have to study for a test.	D You want to stay up late, but you have to get up early.	E You want to meet friends, but you have to take care of your little brother.
YOU	☐	☐	☐	☐	☐
YOUR FRIEND	☐	☐	☐	☐	☐

1 OK   2 not very frustrating   3 somewhat frustrating   4 frustrating   5 very frustrating

HOME SCHOOL LINK

You want to play video games, but you have to do homework.

It's frustrating, but I'm OK about it. What about you?

Tell your family how to be flexible about things.

Lesson 6   Can understand details of a story / Can talk about how flexible I am

18 Read and write the missing words. Then listen and check.

> airport   beaches   island   online   places   school

From: alex@yoohoo.com
To: sun_kwan@nmail.com

Hi Sun-kwan,
I'm writing to you because I want to have an
¹_____ friend in a big city! I love sending emails to friends.
I live in a village on Sark. Sark is a very small British
²_____ near France. Only 600 people live on Sark. I'm happy here because my family and friends are here. I love school, too. There's only one ³_____ on Sark, and we sometimes play sports, but often there aren't many people to make teams.
The ⁴_____ here are very clean, and they're very quiet. There are two banks, but there aren't any shopping malls on the island. We have to go by boat for an hour to another island to go shopping! On Sark, there isn't an
⁵_____, and there aren't any cars. We ride our bikes everywhere. It's really quiet here.
I want to make new friends from different ⁶_____.
Do you like living in Seoul?
Please email me soon. I want to know about your life in a big city!
Alex

Alex

Sun-kwan

19 Answer the questions.

1   What does Alex love doing?
    He loves _____.
2   Why is Alex happy to live on Sark?
    Because _____.
3   Where does Alex go shopping?
    He _____.
4   Why is Alex writing to Sun-kwan?
    _____

20 Imagine you live in a special place. Ask and answer about it.

1   Where is your special place?
2   What things can you do there?
3   What do you like about it?

Lesson 7

Can understand an email about living on an island

21 ⭐ **What do you know?**

GEOGRAPHY 3

22 🎧 **Listen and read. Where are the places in the pictures?**

Cool places

There are some very interesting cities, towns, and villages in the world. Here are some of them. Which do you want to see?

Barcelona, Spain
Look at these beautiful chimneys! They are on the roof of a house in Barcelona. They are by Antoni Gaudi. Gaudi was a famous Spanish architect.
This is a nice place to sit, but it is noisy in the summer. It is in a big park, and it looks like a snake! Its name is the Serpentine Bench.

Bourton-on-the-Hill and Bourton-on-the-Water, England
One of these villages is on a hill, and the other is on a river. In Bourton-on-the-Water, there are little bridges over the river. There are a lot of wonderful, old villages in England. They are usually quiet but beautiful.

Alice Springs, Australia
Alice Springs is a town in the middle of the desert. A lot of tourists want to visit Alice Springs because the world-famous Uluru, or Ayers Rock, is near the town.

23 **Circle.**

1. The chimneys by Antoni Gaudi are in (Spain / the United Kingdom).
2. The Serpentine Bench is (next to a museum / in a park).
3. Bourton-on-the-Water is (on a river / next to the ocean).
4. Alice Springs is (a rock / a town).

MINI PROJECT

24 **Find out about an interesting place. Then write.**

- **Ideas** – Choose a famous place anywhere in the world.
- **Plan** – Make detailed notes about it.
  Where is it? What's there? Who lives there? What can you do there? Is it noisy/quiet/beautiful/hot, etc.? Why do you like it?
- **Write** – Use your notes. Write a paragraph about the place.
- **Share** – Tell a classmate about the famous place that you chose.

Lesson 8 — Can understand a text about cool places / Can find out and write about an interesting place

25 Listen and number.

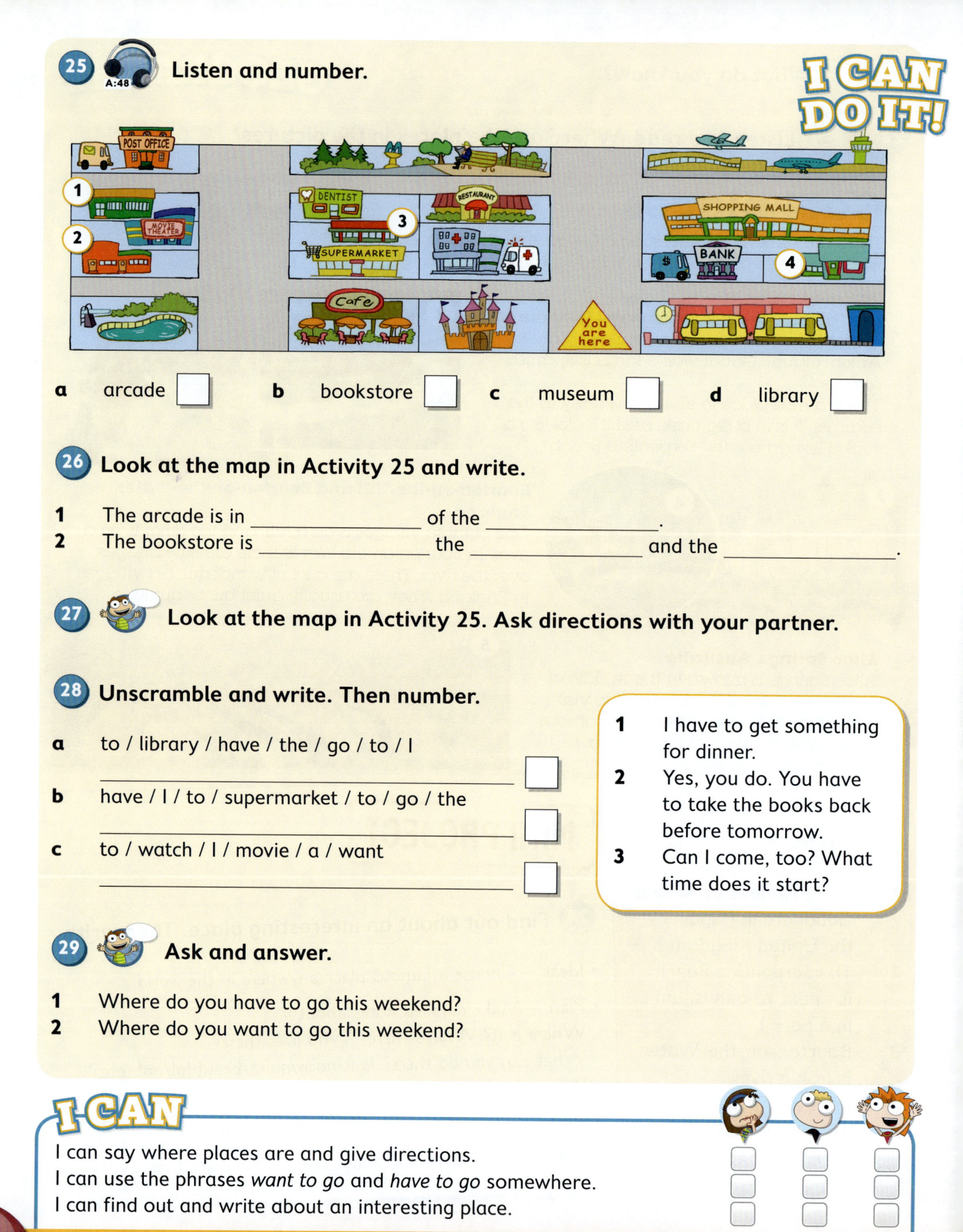

a arcade ☐   b bookstore ☐   c museum ☐   d library ☐

26 Look at the map in Activity 25 and write.

1 The arcade is in _____ of the _____.
2 The bookstore is _____ the _____ and the _____.

27 Look at the map in Activity 25. Ask directions with your partner.

28 Unscramble and write. Then number.

a to / library / have / the / go / to / I
   _____ ☐

b have / I / to / supermarket / to / go / the
   _____ ☐

c to / watch / I / movie / a / want
   _____ ☐

1 I have to get something for dinner.
2 Yes, you do. You have to take the books back before tomorrow.
3 Can I come, too? What time does it start?

29 Ask and answer.

1 Where do you have to go this weekend?
2 Where do you want to go this weekend?

I CAN

I can say where places are and give directions.
I can use the phrases *want to go* and *have to go* somewhere.
I can find out and write about an interesting place.

Lesson 9

Can assess what I have learned in Unit 3

Puzzle!

HAVE FUN 3

30 Where do you want to go?

1 Read the hints.

- Z is the first letter.
- G is next to I.
- P is between R and S.
- A is between B and C.
- J is between K and L.
- V is between U and X.
- D is between E and F.
- M is between N and O.
- W is the last letter.

2 Write the letters.

A	B	C	D	E	F	G	H	I	J	K	L	M
1	2	3	4	5	6	7	8	9	10	11	12	13
	B		C	E			F	H I		K		L

N	O	P	Q	R	S	T	U	V	W	X	Y	Z
14	15	16	17	18	19	20	21	22	23	24	25	26
N		O	Q	R		S	T	U		X	Y	

3 Change the numbers to letters.

4 Find and cross out the place names, i.e. school.

5 Write the letters that are left over.

_____

_____

6 Unscramble these letters. Where do you want to go?

_____

19	16	20	21	16	7	7	9	4	5
20	13	4	21	8	9	20	2	20	20
4	9	3	2	16	21	21	16	26	8
8	2	20	3	20	18	3	16	9	16
16	18	21	11	19	3	6	11	15	19
16	3	13	5	9	19	9	20	15	19
13	18	5	18	21	3	22	21	9	9
15	25	5	25	3	18	15	16	14	14
2	3	14	11	13	11	5	18	10	10
20	21	3	21	9	16	14	5	19	15
16	3	9	18	19	16	18	21	16	3
7	3	4	21	16	18	25	8	16	13
5	3	18	4	3	6	5	23	13	13
18	5	20	21	3	22	18	3	14	21

31 What did you enjoy in this unit? What do you want to know more about?

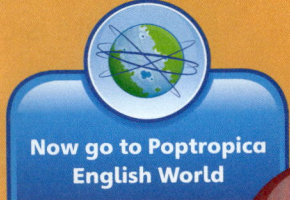

Now go to Poptropica English World

Lesson 10

Can use what I have learned in Unit 3

45

Wider World 2
Our homes

1 ⭐ What do you know?

2 🗨 Look at pictures a–c and make sentences.

There are a lot of white houses.

a

b

3 🎧 A:49 Listen and read. Then number the pictures in Activity 2.

1 I'm from a small town in Andalucía, Spain. My house is very unusual. It's a cave house. Some people think caves are scary and dark, but I think they're great. There are a lot of nice places to visit in my town. A lot of people go to the beautiful beaches on the weekend. It's fun to play volleyball on the sand. The old castles near my house are very interesting, too. My favorite is called Vèlez-Blanco. I love my home!

Alba, 11, Spain

2 I live in Hong Kong, a very busy place in China. Seven million people live in Hong Kong. It's very noisy here, but it's never boring. I live on the fortieth floor of a building in Kowloon. It has great views. There's a sports center behind our apartment. I go there every day to learn taekwondo. There are a lot of shopping malls, restaurants, and museums near my home. The science museum is my favorite. I always learn new and interesting things there. I love Hong Kong!

Chiu-Wai, 12, China

4 Circle.

1 Alba lives in a (cave house / beach house) in Spain.
2 She likes going to the (museum / beach) on the weekend.
3 There's a (supermarket / sports center) behind Chiu-Wai's apartment.
4 Chiu-Wai is learning (taekwondo / sailing).
5 Eleni lives (near a river / on an island).
6 Eleni's father is (not good at / good at) fishing.

5  Ask and answer.

1 Where do you want to live and why?
2 What do you like about where you live?
3 What don't you like about where you live?

3

I live on an island in Greece called Paros. I live with my family in a beautiful white house in a village. The island is quite small — just 13,000 people live here. There's a harbor near our house. My sister and I like going there and watching the boats. We like sailing, and sometimes we go fishing with our father. My father loves fishing, but he's not very good! I love living on an island.

Eleni, 12, Greece

YOUR TURN!

Draw your ideal town or city. Then write about it.

What's the town's name?
Where is it?
What does it look like?
What's it like living there?
What are your favorite places?

4 Good days, bad days

1 ⭐ Do you know any food dishes from other countries?

2 🎧 A:50 Listen and read. Is Tom happy?

1. Tom, it's dinnertime.
   Good, I'm really hungry!

2. This afternoon I wanted an omelet, but there weren't any eggs. Hannah used them at lunchtime!

3. Then I wanted some spaghetti. But the birds were eating it in front of the tent!

4. I made some noodles, but then I dropped them on the grass!

5. Don't worry. I cooked a big stew for dinner. Come on. Let's go.
   Yum! Thanks!

3 🎧 A:51 Listen and say.

1. curry
2. an omelet
3. spaghetti
4. fish and chips
5. paella
6. dumplings
7. sushi
8. stew
9. rice and beans
10. noodles
11. soup

4 Do you like these food dishes? Ask and answer.

A: Do you like curry?
B: Yes, I do.

A: When did you last eat it?
B: I ate curry last week.

Lesson 1

Can identify food dishes from other countries

5 Listen and number the events in order. Then say.

LOOK!
I **cooked** stew.
He **dropped** the plate.
She **paddled** very quickly.
We **fell** in the lake.

6 Look at Activity 5 and write.

1 Maria _____.
2 Tom _____.
3 They _____.
4 Hannah _____.
5 They _____.

TIP! Use the verb list on pages 115–118 to help you learn past forms of verbs.

7 Write and say.   climbed   dropped   fell   sailed   wanted

1 Yesterday, I _____ a plate in the kitchen.
2 Last week, we _____ new bikes, but my mom said, "No!"
3 A year ago, he _____ Mount Everest.
4 In 2004, she _____ around the world.
5 Last month, I _____ in the river when I was fishing.

8 Talk to a friend about yesterday/last week/last month.

What did you do?
I cooked spaghetti!

Lesson 2 Can talk about things that happened in the past   49

VOCABULARY

9 Listen and circle ✓ or ✗.
Listen again and say.

1. pack my bag — ✓ / ✗
2. miss the bus — ✓ / ✗
3. pass a test — ✓ / ✗
4. eat my lunch — ✓ / ✗
5. bring my juice — ✓ / ✗
6. drop the ball — ✓ / ✗

SONG

10 Listen to the song and write.

Chorus:
It was a bad day, it was really bad.
But you smiled at me, now I'm not sad.
I ^{1}_____ my school bag and walked up the street.
I ^{2}_____ the bus, "Ow, my tired feet."
I didn't ^{3}_____ my test, I was late for class.
My friends said, "Next time, get here fast."
I opened my lunchbox, and said, "No way!"
I didn't ^{4}_____ my juice today.
(Chorus)
I went to the park and played with a ball.
I kicked it too hard; it went over a wall.
A boy helped me, he didn't say his name.
We played baseball in the park and enjoyed the game.
I ^{5}_____ the ball. He said, "That's OK."
Now he's my new friend, and it was a good day.

11 Correct the mistakes.

1. She didn't miss the bus. _____
2. She passed her test. _____
3. He didn't drop the ball. _____

12 Ask and answer about the song.

Did she bring her juice?
What did she do in the park?

50 **Lesson 3**   Can talk about what somebody did and didn't do

SKILLS 4

LOOK!

What happened?

I **didn't pass** my test **because I didn't study**.

He **didn't bring** his juice **because he was late** for school.

13 Write. Then say.

1. We _____ because we were sad. (not laugh)
2. She _____ her eyes because it was a scary movie. (not open)
3. They _____ a second soccer game because they weren't tired. (play)
4. I _____ the test because I studied a lot. (pass)
5. He _____ the bus because he was early. (not miss)

14 Listen and match. Then say.

1. Jenny   2. Jackie and Kari   3. Miki and Sam   4. Mike   5. Ken and Rob

a   b   c   d   e

15 Write. Then say.

1. She _____ the ball because the sun was in her eyes.
2. They _____ the test because they didn't study hard.
3. They _____ in the ocean because there was a red flag.
4. He _____ the curry because he doesn't like spicy food.
5. They _____ soccer because it was too hot.

16 Ask and answer. What didn't you do? Why?

I didn't play soccer because I was tired.

Lesson 4   Can give reasons for things that did and didn't happen using *because*

17 　Talk about the pictures. Then listen and read.　**STORY**

1 ZEB AND DOT ARE AT THE RESTAURANT GASTRONOME.

"Mm, these dumplings are delicious! Did you make them?"

"Why yes, I did."

2 "It's Dot Martin!"

"What is she looking for?"

3 "Eek! It's a rat!"

"It isn't a rat. It's a meerkat!"

4 "This is really good."

"Ah, I needed that."

"Um, where did the Martins go?"

5 "What happened?"

"I only got one because those kids and that RAT stopped me."

"It's not a RAT!"

6 "Did they just take a trash can of old food?"

18 　Why do you think Zeb and Dot want trash cans? Discuss your answers.

19 Circle. Then say.

1. Dot Martin (ate / didn't eat) dumplings.
2. Matt (ate / didn't eat) dumplings.
3. AL (needed / didn't need) oil.
4. Matt (thought / didn't think) the Martins took a trash can.
5. Dot Martin (said / didn't say) the meerkat was a rat.

20 Check (✓) the best summary of the story.

1. Matt and Bella were very hungry. They didn't find the Martins at the restaurant.
2. Everybody ate delicious food at the restaurant. Bella saw a rat.
3. Matt and his friends ate delicious food at the restaurant. Dot and Zeb took a trash can.

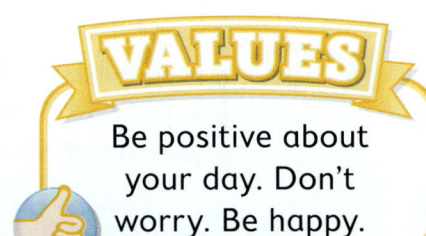

21 Role-play the story.

22 How do you relax after a bad day? Write *always*, *often*, *sometimes*, or *never*. Then ask and answer.

VALUES
Be positive about your day. Don't worry. Be happy.

	You	Your friend
1 Practice a sport.		
2 Watch TV or play video games.		
3 Go online and talk to a friend.		
4 Write a blog post describing your day.		
5 Talk to a family member.		
6 Other?		

I always go online and talk to a friend. What about you?

I often go online and talk to a friend, but I always talk to a family member.

HOME SCHOOL LINK Ask your family members how they relax after a bad day.

Lesson 6 — Can understand details of a story / Can talk about how I relax after a bad day

23 Listen and read. Write the missing words. Then number the pictures.

didn't want   good day   last year   liked   looked   played

My good day

1 One Saturday last May was a great day for me. I played the guitar in a school concert. I was scared. I ᵃ_____ to play. Then I went on stage, and I was OK. I really ᵇ_____ it! Now I want to be a rock star!
Jake, 12

2 My cousin's wedding ᶜ_____ was wonderful. There were a lot of people – about a hundred! The food was great. There was some tasty fish and a tall cake. I didn't want to wear a pink dress, but it ᵈ_____ good on me. Now pink is my favorite color!
Laura, 13

3 Last Friday was a really ᵉ_____. After school, I went to the park with my friends, and we played basketball. Then a group of girls from another school joined us, and we ᶠ_____ together. It was fun!
Sandy, 12

24 Circle T = True or F = False. Then say.

1 Jake wanted to play on stage.   T / F
2 Jake played the guitar.   T / F
3 There was curry at the wedding.   T / F
4 Laura didn't want to wear a pink dress.   T / F
5 Sandy played soccer in the park last Friday.   T / F
6 A group of girls from Sandy's school joined her.   T / F

> False! He didn't want to play on stage.

25 Answer the questions.

1 Why was Jake's day great?
   Because _____.

2 Why is pink now Laura's favorite color?
   _____

3 Who played basketball with Sandy?
   _____

Lesson 7   Can understand texts about other children's good days

SOCIAL SCIENCE **4**

26 ⭐ What do you know?

27 🎧 Listen and read. What did Ellen do in 2005? What was good/bad?
A:61

Amazing Ellen

Ellen MacArthur is a famous British sailor who sailed alone around the world and broke the world record.

1 The Race Around the World

Ellen's race started in November 2004 and finished in February 2005. She broke the world record by 33 hours. She became the fastest person to sail around the world alone. When Ellen was at sea, she filmed her journey. We can see her good and bad days on her videos.

2 Bad Times in the Race

It was often dangerous, but Ellen was brave. There were storms and big waves. Her food was boring and dry, and she was often tired. One very bad day for Ellen was Christmas Day. There was a big storm, and it was scary. Ellen called her family, but she didn't want to talk. She didn't open her Christmas presents.

3 A Good Time in the Race

New Year's Day was good for Ellen. There were no storms. Ellen called her friends and family. She opened her Christmas presents, seven days late, and laughed. There were some funny presents. She enjoyed that day.

28 Circle.

1 Ellen started her race in (November / December) 2004.
2 She finished in (2005 / 2006).
3 It was (never / often) dangerous.
4 Ellen (enjoyed / didn't enjoy) Christmas Day 2004.
5 Ellen (called / didn't call) her family on New Year's Day.

MINI PROJECT

29 Choose a famous sportsperson. Write about a special thing they did.

- **Ideas** — Choose a sportsperson who did something very special.
- **Plan** — Make detailed notes about him/her. What did he/she do? When/Where did he/she do it? What was difficult/special about it?
- **Write** — Use your notes. Write a paragraph.
- **Share** — Tell a classmate about your sportsperson's success story.

Lesson 8 — Can understand a text about a famous sailor / Can write about a famous sportsperson

30 Listen and check (✓) two items.

What happened?	a	b	c
1 Mandy			
2 Greg			
3 Joan			

31 Answer the questions.

1. What happened after Mandy was late? _____
2. Why was Greg hungry at lunchtime? _____
3. What made Joan unhappy? _____

32 Match.

1. This is a kind of fried food.
2. You want something to drink.
3. This is fish that is not cooked.
4. Study hard to do this.
5. Don't do this before school.
6. This is an Italian food.

a spaghetti
b miss the bus
c fish and chips
d sushi
e bring my juice
f pass a test

33 Ask and answer.

1. What is your favorite food from another country? Why?
2. Tell me what you did and didn't do this week.
3. Tell me about a very good day in your life.

I CAN

I can talk about things that happened in the past.
I can give reasons for things that did and didn't happen using *because*.
I can write about a famous sportsperson.

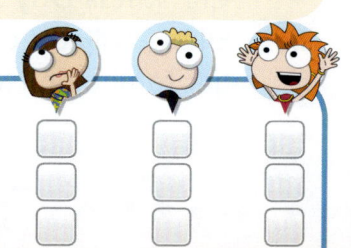

Lesson 9

34. Answer the questions about you. Then interview your friend. Use a time expression from the box. Write your answers. Which pair of students in the class can complete the table first?

HAVE FUN

last month   last week
last year   yesterday

YOU	YOUR FRIEND	YOU	YOUR FRIEND
brush your teeth?		something you ate	
Yes, I did.	No, he didn't.	I ate a	He ate some
do your homework?		something you drank	
wash the dishes?			
cook the lunch?		something you did	
climb a tree?			
		something you didn't do	
play an instrument?			
watch TV?		something you saw	
pass a test?			
		something you didn't want to do	
help a friend?			

Did you brush your teeth yesterday?

No, I didn't.

What did you/didn't you do last week?

I went to school.

35. What did you enjoy in this unit? What do you want to know more about?

Now go to Poptropica English World

Lesson 10

Can use what I have learned in Unit 4   57

Review Units 3 and 4

1 Ask and answer. You are in the music store.

1. How do I get to the station?
2. I want to go to the movie theater. Where is it?
3. How do I get to the supermarket?
4. I want to go to the swimming pool. Where is it?
5. How do I get to the library?
6. I want to go to the children's park. Where is it?

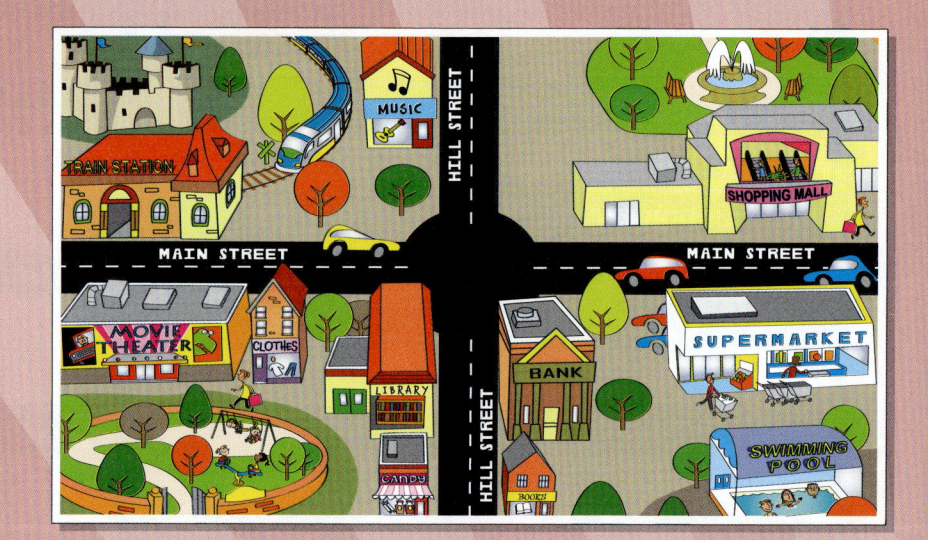

2 Choose three more places on the map. Ask and answer.

3 Write. Then say.

> She wants to go to the station.

1. she / want / station
2. they / have / swimming pool
   _____
3. he / want / hospital
   _____

4 Write about yourself.

1. What do you have to do today?
   _____
2. What do you want to do today?
   _____

5 Look and write.

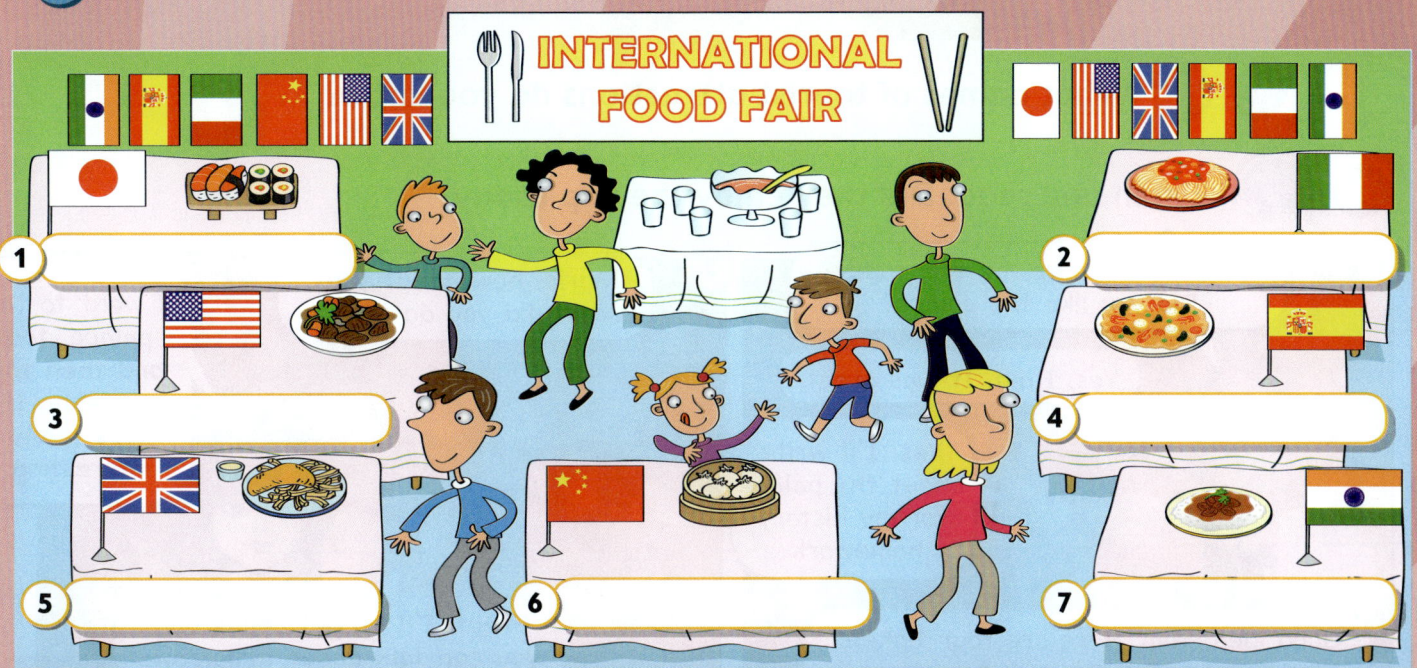

INTERNATIONAL FOOD FAIR

1. _____
2. _____
3. _____
4. _____
5. _____
6. _____
7. _____

6 Imagine you are at the food fair. Write. Then say.

First, I want to eat _____.
Second, I want to eat _____.
Third, I want to eat _____.

7 Write the opposite.

1   I liked the movie last night.
    <u>I didn't like the movie last night.</u>

2   He didn't climb a mountain last year.
    _____

3   Yesterday, we didn't stay at the library all afternoon.
    _____

4   James visited his grandparents last Saturday.
    _____

5   Sally didn't walk to school yesterday.
    _____

6   We played soccer in the park last weekend.
    _____

5 Trips

1 ⭐ What names of tourist attractions do you know?

2 🎧 Listen and read. Did they enjoy the trip today?

1
- Hi! Did you enjoy the trip today? Did you like the palace?
- Yes, I did. It was great.
- Yes. I'll write about the palace for my history homework.
- Good idea, Tom. Here are four tickets for the amusement park tomorrow.

2
- Maria, how about you? What did you do today?
- I went to the palace, too, and then the museum. It was really interesting.
- Great. I'll go get Felipe and you can talk about tomorrow.

3
- Hi, Felipe. We're planning tomorrow now. What will you do at the amusement park?
- I think I'll go on the water slide first.
- Yeah, me too!

3 🎧 Listen and say.

1. aquarium
2. amusement park
3. palace
4. water park
5. theater
6. national park
7. circus
8. botanical gardens

4 Look at Activity 2. Where did Flo, Tom, and Maria go?

60 Lesson 1 — Can identify tourist attractions

LOOK!

What **did you do** yesterday?	**I went** to the aquarium.
Did you go to the aquarium?	Yes, **I did**. / No, **I didn't**.
Did you like the aquarium?	

5 Listen and circle.

1. Did Maria go to Buckingham Palace? (Yes, she did. / No, she didn't.)
2. Did Maria go to the aquarium? (Yes, she did. / No, she didn't.)
3. Did Maria go to the theater? (Yes, she did. / No, she didn't.)
4. Did Maria go to an Indian restaurant? (Yes, she did. / No, she didn't.)

6 Imagine a trip. Write and circle.

1. a I went to the _____. Did you like it? ✓ / ✗
   b _____ Did you like it? ✓ / ✗
   c _____ Did you like it? ✓ / ✗
2. a I didn't go to the _____.
   b _____
   c _____

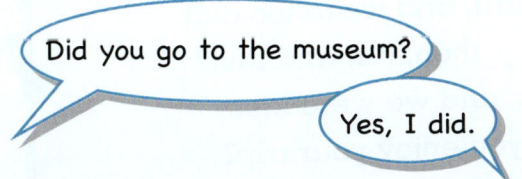

7 Look at Activity 6. Ask and answer about your trip.

- Did you go to the museum?
- Yes, I did.
- Did you like the museum?
- Yes, I did.

8 Ask and answer. What did you do last weekend?

- Did you go to the park?
- No, I didn't.

Lesson 2

Can ask and answer about trips in the past

9 Listen and circle ✓ or ✗. Listen again and say.

VOCABULARY

1. ride the Ferris wheel ✓ / ✗
2. go on the bumper cars ✓ / ✗
3. play miniature golf ✓ / ✗
4. go on the paddle boats ✓ / ✗
5. ride the roller coaster ✓ / ✗
6. go on the pirate ship ✓ / ✗
7. go on the water slide ✓ / ✗

10 Listen to the song and write.

SONG

We went to an ¹ _____ yesterday.
A special treat for my brother's birthday.
Did you like the ² _____, going up high?
Yes, I did! Because I can fly!
Did you like the carousel with horses of gold?
No, we didn't! The horses were small, and we're too old!
Did you like the ³ _____ then, fun and fast?
No, we didn't! Our car was slow, and we were last.
So what rides did you like? Did you enjoy your trip?
Did you like the ⁴ _____ and the ⁵ _____?
Yes, and we loved the ⁶ _____, it was so quick.
We went on it ten times, and now we feel sick.

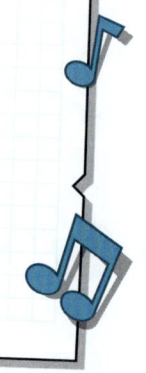

11 Look at Activity 10. Ask and answer.

- Did they like the bumper cars?
- No, they didn't.
- Why didn't they like them?
- Because their car was slow.

Lesson 3

SKILLS 5

LOOK!

What **will you do** at the amusement park?
First, **I'll ride** the Ferris wheel. Then **I'll go** on the bumper cars.

12 Listen and number. Then ask and answer.

What will you do at the amusement park?

First, I'll ride the Ferris wheel. Then I'll go on the pirate ship.

1 a   b
2 a   b
3 a   b

13 Look at Activity 12 and write.

1 First, I'll _____.
  Then I'll _____.
2 First, _____.
  Then _____.
3 _____
  _____

14 Ask and answer. What will you do next week/summer/winter/year?

Lesson 4 — Can ask and answer about planned activities

15 Talk about the pictures. Then listen and read.

STORY

AT THE AMUSEMENT PARK

1. Wow. What happened here?
Ooh! Rides!
I'll tell you what happened! Those weird guys... Grrr!

2. They wanted to go on the ride. They went into a pod.

3. The door closed, then I saw a flash, and there was a BANG. And then the pod took off.

4. But these pods can't fly, can they?
Well, this one certainly flew. It flew right off the ride!

5. Where did it fly?
HOW did it fly?
Hmm, maybe they used the THD for power.

6. Well, it didn't work. Look.
I don't understand. What do those weird guys want?

16 Why do you think Carol and Matt say that Dot and Zeb are "weird"?

Lesson 5 — Can understand a simple story / Can discuss a story

17 Write. Then number the story events in order.

> amusement park   Bella   flash   pod   ride

☐ Carol Carnival saw a _____ and heard a bang.
☐ The _____ flew off the ride.
☐ _____ found the pod in the lake.
☐ Matt, Bell, and Al arrived in the _____.
☐ Dot and Zeb Martin went on a _____.

18 Imagine you are Carol or Matt. Ask and answer.

> What happened today?

> Two weird guys...

VALUES
Plan, but be flexible. Planning helps you do more things.

19 Role-play the story.

20 Write in the schedule below to plan your day. Then share with a friend.

Saturday		
Time	To do	How long?
7:30	get up, shower, and have breakfast	1 hour

> I think I will get up, shower, and have breakfast at 7:30.

> I will get up, shower, and have breakfast at 7:00.

HOME SCHOOL LINK
Help a family member to plan his/her day.

Lesson 6

21 Listen and read. Then match the underlined words to the pictures.

Hawaii is the place to be!

a
b
c
d

Fantastic sandy beaches (**1**), great ocean, and lots to do! Go surfing (**2**), sailing, or paragliding (**3**)! Visit the Waikiki Aquarium or the Wet 'n' Wild water park! At night, see a concert or try Hawaiian dancing (**4**)! There's something for the whole family!

August 14th
Hi Gemma,
I'm in Hawaii. It's great! On the first day, we went surfing. The ocean was warm, but surfing was difficult. I'll try it again tomorrow. We also went paragliding. It was exciting flying in the air! Yesterday it rained, but today it was hot, and it didn't rain. We played volleyball on the beach. The aquarium was good, and I really loved the sea turtles and the fish. We also visited the water park. It was a great vacation, and I want to come back next year. Are you enjoying your summer vacation, too? What did you do? Where did you go? I'll see you when I get back.
Love,
Sarah

22 Is Hawaii a good place for a vacation? What can you do there? Discuss.

23 Imagine you went on vacation last summer. Write.

TIP!
Last summer,... On the first day,... Then...
I/We was/were (in/at)... I/We went... I/We saw...
I/We liked/didn't like... I/We visited/played...

Hi, _____,
I'm in _____.
_____
_____
_____
Love,
_____

Lesson 7 Can understand and write a letter about a vacation in Hawaii

SOCIAL SCIENCE 5

24 ⭐ What do you know?

25 🎧 Listen and read. What do the different flags mean?

BEACH SAFETY IN AUSTRALIA

1 Sun safety
- Put on some clothes – always wear a T-shirt or other clothes.
- Put on sunblock – always wear sunblock in the sun.
- Put on a hat – always wear a hat to cover your head in the sun.

2 Swim safety
- Swim between the red and yellow flags. This water is safe.
- Never swim near a red flag. It means the water is dangerous.
- Always swim near the beach. Don't swim far away.

3 Surf safety
- Always surf between the surfing signs.
- Always stay with your surfboard.
- Never surf between blue flags.

MINI PROJECT

27 Make a safety poster about a dangerous outdoor activity in your country.

- **Ideas** – Choose an outdoor activity that can be dangerous.
- **Plan** – Make notes. Think of rules that can make it safe.
  Never... Always... Don't forget to...
  You can... You can't... Wear... Take...
- **Write** – Make a poster like in Activity 25.
- **Share** – Show your poster and tell the class about it.

26 Answer the questions.

1. What do you need to wear for sun safety?
   a _____
   b _____
   c _____
2. Where is it dangerous to swim?
   _____
3. Where can you never surf?
   _____

Lesson 8 — Can understand a text about beach safety in Australia / Can make a safety poster — **67**

28 Circle.

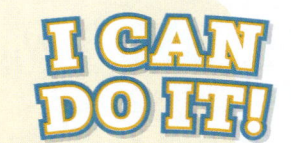

1 Last week, I went on the roller coaster at the
   (water park / castle / amusement park).
2 Yesterday, I went mountain hiking in the (national park / aquarium / palace).
3 First, I'll go on the (Ferris wheel / miniature golf / paddle boats) because I like
   to go up high.
4 Then I'll ride the (pirate ship / roller coaster / bumper cars) because it's very fast.

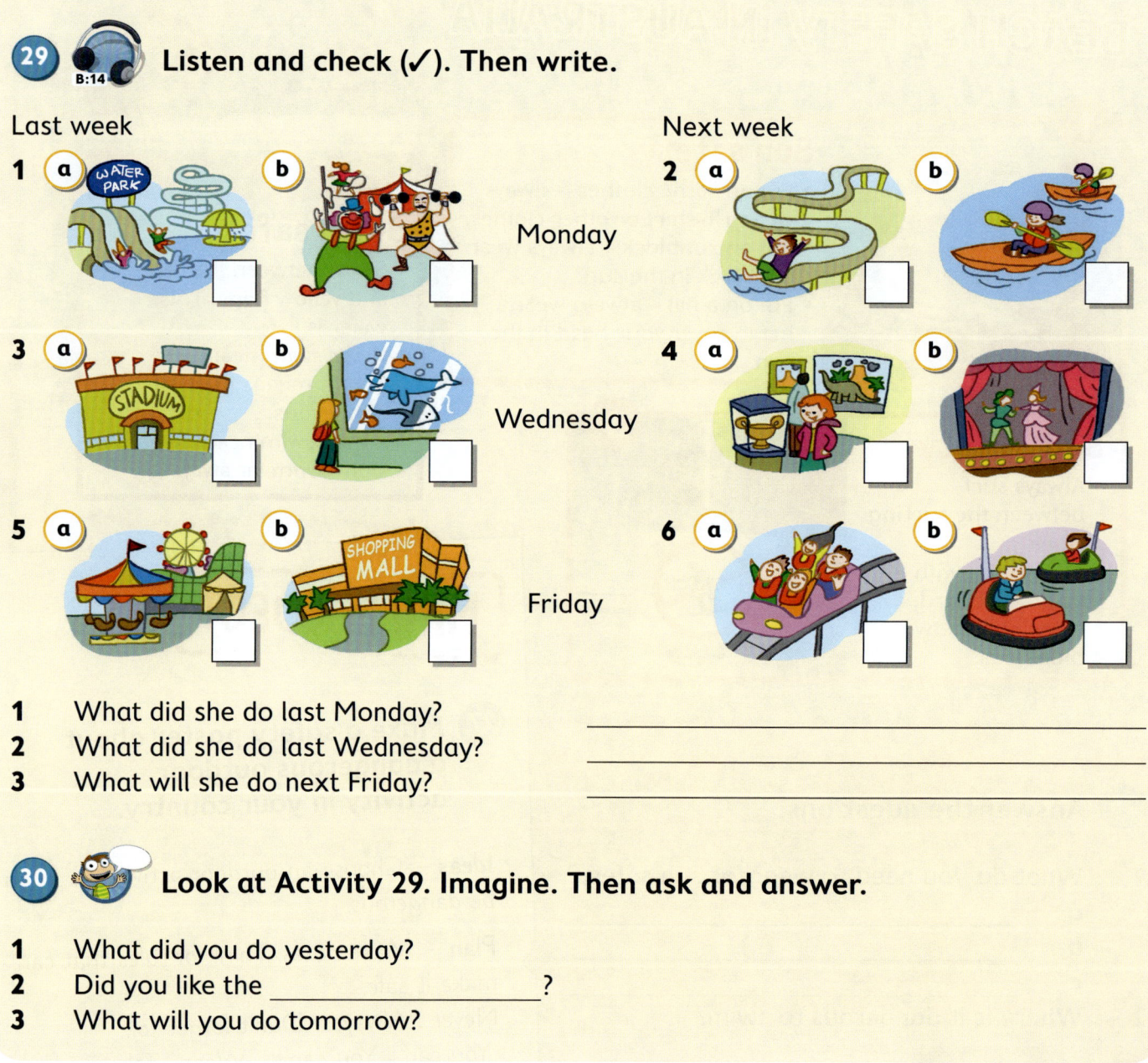

29 Listen and check (✓). Then write.

Last week   **Next week**

1 a b   Monday   2 a b
3 a b   Wednesday 4 a b
5 a b   Friday   6 a b

1 What did she do last Monday?   _____
2 What did she do last Wednesday? _____
3 What will she do next Friday?   _____

30 Look at Activity 29. Imagine. Then ask and answer.

1 What did you do yesterday?
2 Did you like the _____?
3 What will you do tomorrow?

I CAN

I can identify tourist attractions and amusement park activities.
I can ask and answer about planned activities.
I can make a safety poster.

Lesson 9

31 Draw. Then listen to your friend and draw.

HAVE FUN 5

Design an amusement park!

Your amusement park

Your friend's amusement park

The Ferris wheel is next to the entrance.

32 What did you enjoy in this unit? What do you want to know more about?

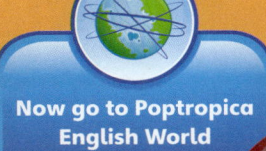

Now go to Poptropica English World

Lesson 10

Can use what I have learned in Unit 5

Wider World 3
Our vacations

1 ⭐ What do you know?

2 Look at pictures a–c and make sentences.

> This place is in the mountains. It looks like an old town.

a

b

3 🎧 B:15 Listen and read. Then number the pictures in Activity 2.

1 Last year, I went to a city called Agra in India. I visited the Taj Mahal with my family. A man called Emperor Shah Jahan married a princess called Mumtaz Mahal. When she died, he was very sad. He built the Taj Mahal for her. Twenty thousand workers used one thousand elephants and finished it in 1653. The tombs of Emperor Shah Jahan and his wife are inside the Taj Mahal. I think the Taj Mahal is beautiful!

Samir, 11, India

2 This summer, I went by bus to an ancient city in Turkey called Cappadocia. We stayed in a hotel in front of the Uçhisar Castle. During the day, we visited a city that was inside a mountain. There are houses, restaurants, and hotels all inside the mountain. We then went in a hot-air balloon and saw the beautiful Fairy Chimneys. After that, we visited a famous Turkish bath. I can't wait to visit Cappadocia again next year.

Zara, 12, Turkey

4 **Circle T = True or F = False.**

1. The Taj Mahal is in India. T / F
2. There aren't any tombs inside the Taj Mahal. T / F
3. Zara's hotel was inside a castle. T / F
4. You can visit a Turkish bath at Cappadocia. T / F
5. People called Andes lived in Machu Picchu long ago. T / F
6. The Intihuatana Stone was a sundial. T / F

5 **Ask and answer.**

1. What was your favorite vacation?
2. What's a nice place to visit where you live?

3 Last year, I visited a city called Machu Picchu. It's in the Andes mountains in Peru. Long ago, people called Incas lived in this ancient city. The city was lost in the mountains for hundreds of years. There are ruins of gardens, houses, and even a palace. My favorite ruin is called the Intihuatana Stone. It was a big sundial at the top of a big pyramid. There were often special celebrations around the Intihuatana Stone. Machu Picchu is a great place to visit!

Juan, 12, Peru

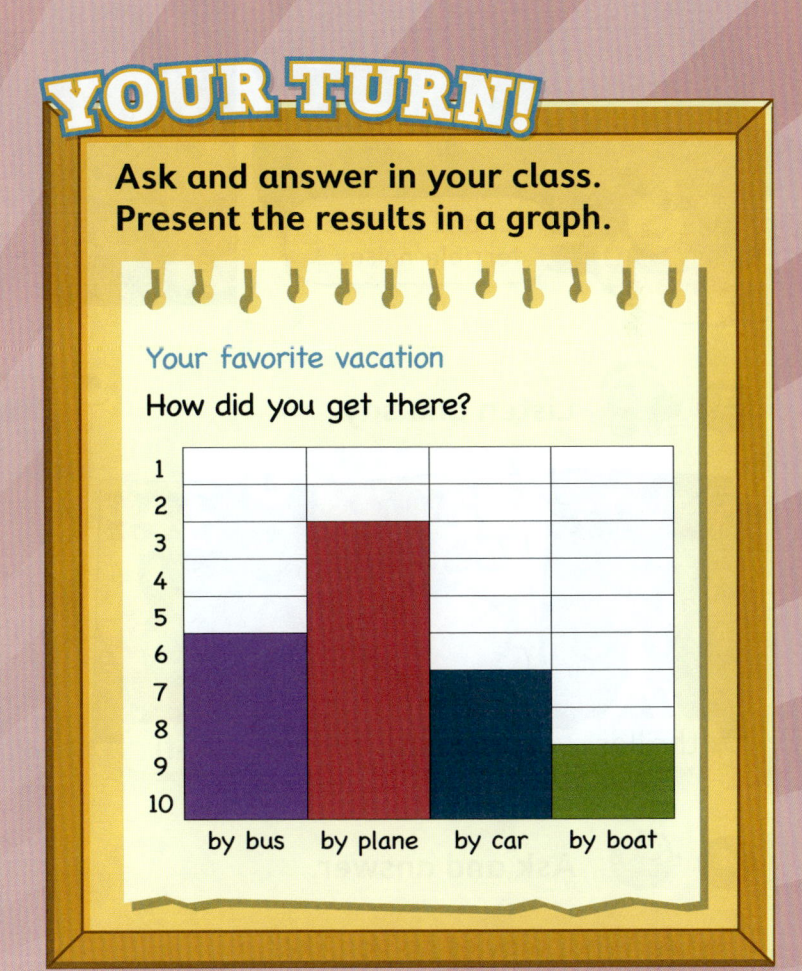

YOUR TURN!

Ask and answer in your class. Present the results in a graph.

Your favorite vacation
How did you get there?

Wider World 3 — Can talk about my favorite vacation

6 Arts

1 ⭐ What different types of movies do you know? Which do you like?

2 🎧 Listen and read. What is *Shadow in the House*?

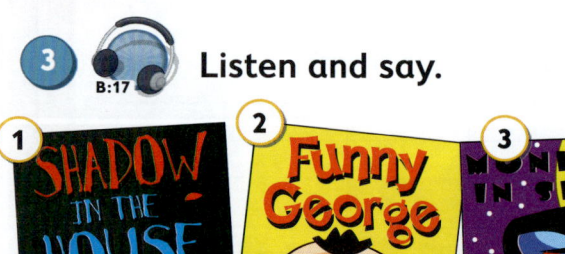

1 Hi, Maria!
Hi, guys! I just saw *Shadow in the House* by myself. It's a scary thriller, but I had a great time!

2 There was something in the house. It wrote letters on the window...

3 ... and it made terrible noises...

4 Boo! Aaah! Flo, we didn't see you!

5 Sorry, Maria!

3 🎧 Listen and say.

1. thriller
2. comedy
3. sci-fi
4. romance
5. musical
6. cartoon
7. action
8. western

4 💬 Ask and answer.

A: What movies do you like?
B: I like thrillers and...

Lesson 1 — Can identify different types of movies

5 Look at Activity 2. Circle T = True or F = False.

1. Maria saw a scary movie.   T / F
2. Maria didn't have a good time.   T / F
3. The shadow didn't write on the window.   T / F
4. Maria didn't see the movie by herself.   T / F
5. Felipe walked to the movie theater by himself.   T / F

LOOK!

I **saw** the movie by **myself**.
You **wrote** it by **yourself**.
He **made** it by **himself**.
She **didn't go** to the movie by **herself**.
We **didn't watch** it by **ourselves**.
They **didn't draw** it by **themselves**.

6 Circle. Then listen and check your answers.

1. I (wrote / didn't write) the letter by myself.
2. The girl (played / didn't play) by herself.
3. They (made / didn't make) dinner by themselves.
4. He (watched / didn't watch) the movie by himself.

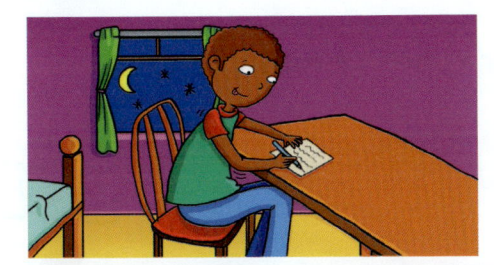

7 Write. Then say.

I wrote my homework last Monday by myself.

1. I _____ my homework last Monday _____. (write/me)
2. You _____ a movie last week _____. (see/you)
3. We _____ a good time last Saturday _____. (have/we)
4. He _____ dinner for his family yesterday _____. (make/he)
5. They _____ karaoke last year _____. (sing/they)

Lesson 2

Can talk about things I did or didn't do *by myself*

VOCABULARY

8 Listen and say. Then listen to the music and number the instrument.

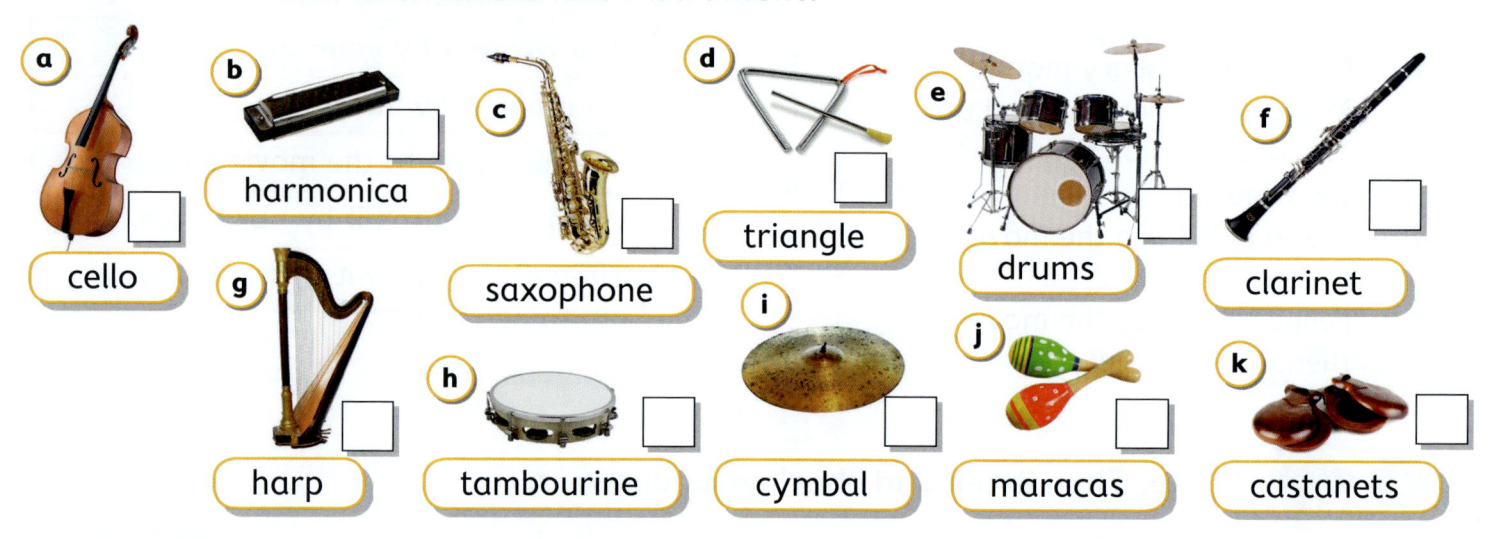

a. cello
b. harmonica
c. saxophone
d. triangle
e. drums
f. clarinet
g. harp
h. tambourine
i. cymbal
j. maracas
k. castanets

9 Listen and say. Do you know any other types of music?

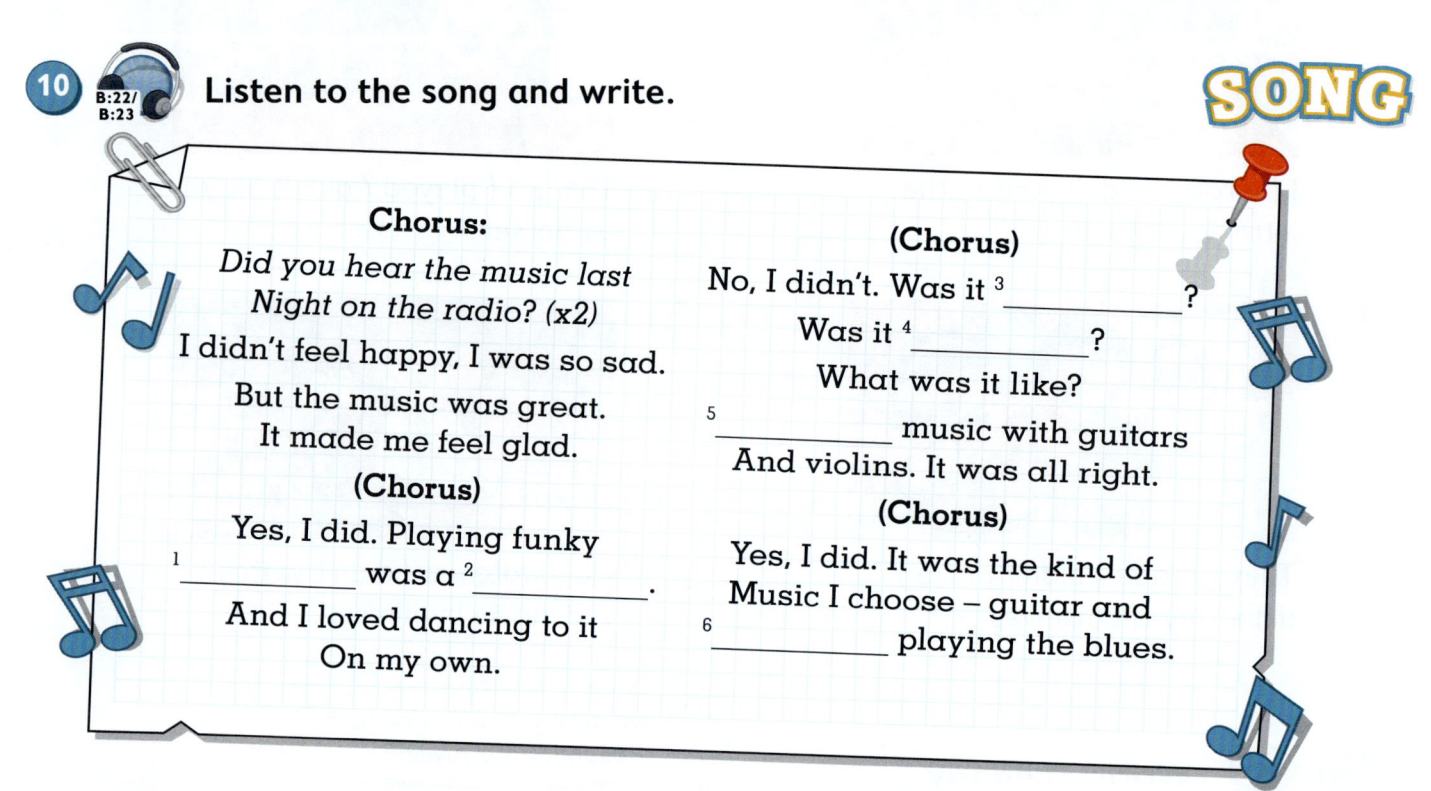

SONG

10 Listen to the song and write.

Chorus:
Did you hear the music last
Night on the radio? (x2)
I didn't feel happy, I was so sad.
But the music was great.
It made me feel glad.
(Chorus)
Yes, I did. Playing funky
¹_____ was a ²_____.
And I loved dancing to it
On my own.

(Chorus)
No, I didn't. Was it ³_____?
Was it ⁴_____?
What was it like?
⁵_____ music with guitars
And violins. It was all right.
(Chorus)
Yes, I did. It was the kind of
Music I choose – guitar and
⁶_____ playing the blues.

11 Listen to the song again and circle.

1. Did you hear the guitar? Y / N
2. Did you hear the saxophone? Y / N
3. Did you hear the violin? Y / N
4. Did you hear the harmonica? Y / N
5. Did you hear the piano? Y / N

12 Ask and answer.

1. see / a concert / last week?
2. make / a cake / on Sunday?
3. say sorry / yesterday?
4. have / a party / last month?
5. sing / a song / last night?

Lesson 3 — Can identify musical instruments

SKILLS 6

LOOK!

Did you hear the cello?	Yes, I did. / No, I didn't.
Have you ever played the saxophone?	Yes, I have. / No, I haven't.
Have you ever been to a concert?	Yes, I have. / No, I've never been to a concert.

13 Listen and check (✓).

TIP!

play	played
go	been
got	gotten
eat	eaten

See more on page 115.

14 Look at Activity 13 and write the questions and your answers. Then ask and answer.

1 Have you _____ 100 percent in a test?
   Your answer: _____
2 Have _____?
   Your answer: _____
3 _____ to another country?
   Your answer: _____
4 _____ in one day?
   Your answer: _____

Lesson 4

Can ask and answer using *Have you ever...?*

15 Talk about the pictures. Then listen and read. **STORY**

1. ZEB AND DOT MARTIN ARE NOT HERE.
Wow! I always wanted to see a recording studio!
There's nobody here.

2. HELP!! BANG BANG

3. Thank you! A man and a woman came. They were weird. They locked me in here.
Did they take anything?

4. They just recorded some music. Hey, they took the saxophone!

5. So, where are they now?
Hmm, they took a trash can of old food and now a saxophone. What's going on?
We have a trace!

6. I wonder what they were recording.
Oh, well.

16 Why do you think Dot and Zeb went to the studio?

Lesson 5 — Can understand a simple story / Can discuss a story

17 Circle.

1. The Martins (locked / hid) Peter up.
2. They (bought / took) a saxophone and (sang / recorded) music. Then they (came / left) again.
3. Matt, AL, and Bella (pushed / helped) Peter. He said the Martins were (smart / weird).
4. Bella (didn't want / wanted) to know where they went. Matt (didn't know / knew) why they took things.
5. AL (found / didn't find) a trace of the Martins.

18 Check (✓).

1. The Martins tried to take a pod…
   - [ ] before they took the trash can.
   - [ ] after they took the trash can.
2. Matt, Bella, and AL went to Africa…
   - [ ] before they went to Atlantis.
   - [ ] after they went to Atlantis.
3. Dot met the meerkat…
   - [ ] before she took a second trash can.
   - [ ] after she took a second trash can.
4. Dot and Zeb recorded some music…
   - [ ] before they locked Peter in a closet.
   - [ ] after they locked Peter in a closet.

19 Role-play the story.

20 Read and write ✓ = by myself or ✓✓✓ = with my friends. Then share with a friend.

	You	Your friend
1 Review for a test.		
2 Go to a concert.		
3 Make a draft of something you are writing.		
4 Find information for a project.		

VALUES

Learn to be self-sufficient. You can always do some things by yourself.

I review for a test by myself.

I review for a test with my friends.

HOME SCHOOL LINK Tell your family about the things you can do by yourself.

Lesson 6 — Can understand details of a story / Can talk about things I do by myself — 77

21 Listen and read. Is the book a thriller, a romance, or a comedy?

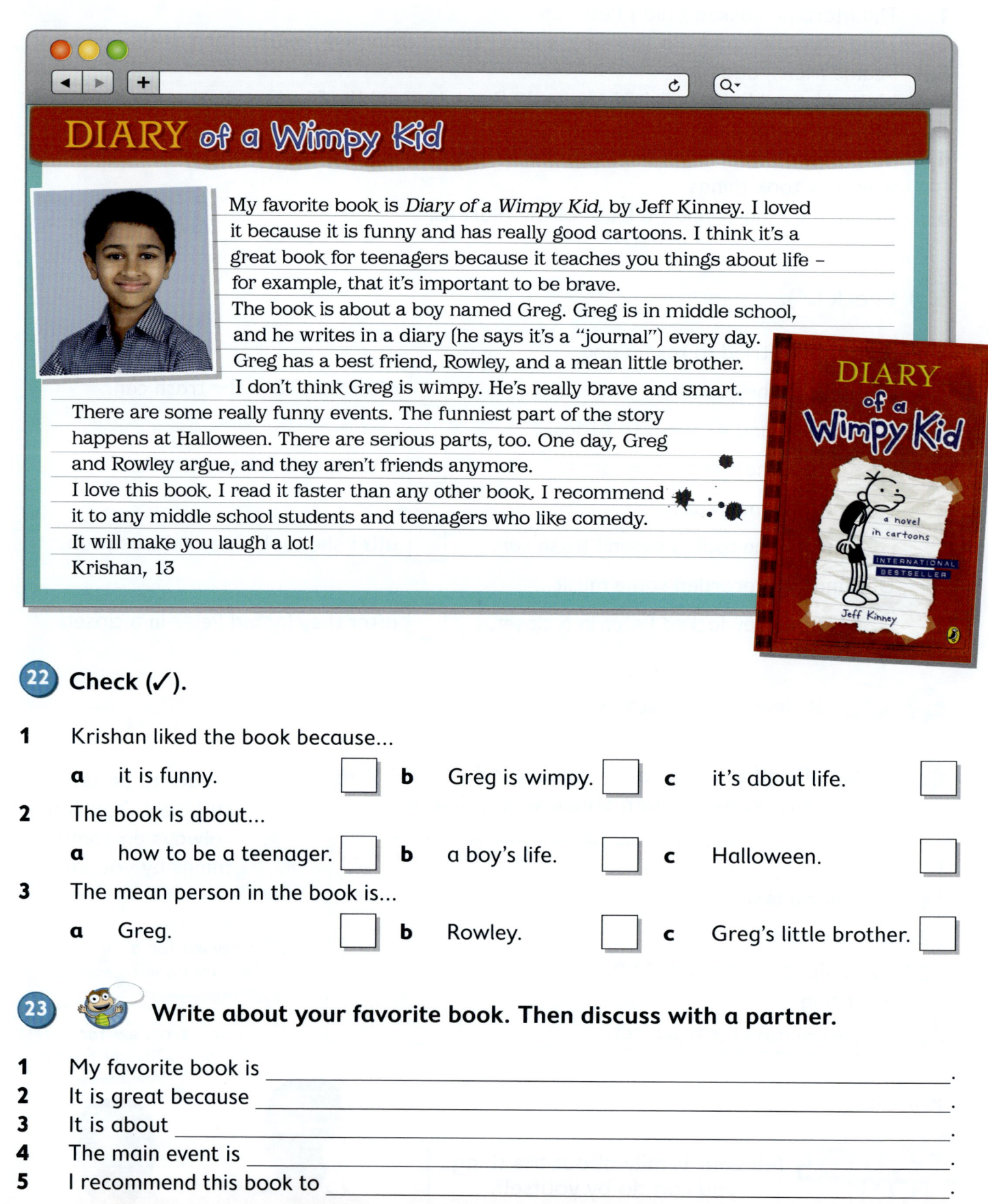

DIARY of a Wimpy Kid

My favorite book is *Diary of a Wimpy Kid*, by Jeff Kinney. I loved it because it is funny and has really good cartoons. I think it's a great book for teenagers because it teaches you things about life – for example, that it's important to be brave.

The book is about a boy named Greg. Greg is in middle school, and he writes in a diary (he says it's a "journal") every day. Greg has a best friend, Rowley, and a mean little brother. I don't think Greg is wimpy. He's really brave and smart.

There are some really funny events. The funniest part of the story happens at Halloween. There are serious parts, too. One day, Greg and Rowley argue, and they aren't friends anymore.

I love this book. I read it faster than any other book. I recommend it to any middle school students and teenagers who like comedy. It will make you laugh a lot!

Krishan, 13

22 Check (✓).

1 Krishan liked the book because…

   a it is funny. ☐   **b** Greg is wimpy. ☐   **c** it's about life. ☐

2 The book is about…

   a how to be a teenager. ☐   **b** a boy's life. ☐   **c** Halloween. ☐

3 The mean person in the book is…

   a Greg. ☐   **b** Rowley. ☐   **c** Greg's little brother. ☐

23 Write about your favorite book. Then discuss with a partner.

1 My favorite book is _____.
2 It is great because _____.
3 It is about _____.
4 The main event is _____.
5 I recommend this book to _____.

Lesson 7

Can understand a text about a favorite book

24 ⭐ What do you know?

25 🎧 Listen and read the poem. Match the questions to the pictures.

LITERATURE 6

Bad Day
By José Luis Morales

On a bad day, bad things happen.
Have you ever failed a test?
Have you ever missed a bus?
Have you ever been afraid?
Have you ever fallen down?
Have you ever scraped your knee?
Have you ever hurt your foot?
Have you ever lost your keys?
Have you ever had a headache?
Have you ever felt real sad?
Have you ever missed a friend?
Have you ever said "That's bad!"?
On a bad day, bad things happen.
Take a deep breath. Count to ten.
Think a good day lies ahead.

That's bad!

Bye!

26 Have any of the things in the poem ever happened to you? How did you feel? What were you doing at the time?

27 Choose three questions from the poem. Ask and answer.

- Have you ever been afraid?
- Yes, I have. I was riding a roller coaster.

MINI PROJECT

28 Write a poem about a good day.

- **Ideas** – Think about good days. What kinds of things happen?
- **Plan** – Make notes. Write as many examples as you can.
- **Write** – Use "Bad Day" as a model. Write a poem! Start: "On a good day, good things happen."
- **Share** – Read your poem out loud to the class.

Lesson 8   Can talk about the poem *Bad Day* / Can write a poem about a good day

29 Circle.

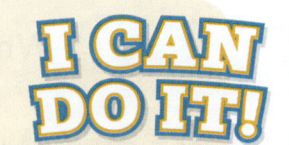

1. I was scared when I watched the (**thriller** / comedy / western) by myself.
2. The (musical / romance / **sci-fi**) movie was set in the year 2078.
3. The saxophone and (the cello / **the clarinet** / the harp) are instruments you play with your mouth.
4. You can play the guitar and the (clarinet / saxophone / **harmonica**) at the same time.

30 Listen and check (✓) two items.

Have you ever...?			
1 Ann	a	b	c
2 Dave	a	b	c
3 Jay	a	b	c

31 Look at Activity 30. Write questions and answers.

1. Has Ann ever flown in a plane by herself? _____
2. _____ sushi? Yes, he has.
3. Did Jay watch a thriller by himself last year? _____

32 Look at Activity 30. Imagine. Then ask and answer.

Have you ever...? Did you...?

I CAN

I can identify different types of movies and musical instruments.
I can talk about things I did or didn't do *by myself*.
I can write a poem about a good day.

Lesson 9

HAVE FUN 6

33 Answer the questions. Then tell your partner your answers. Your partner has to guess the question.

Guess the Question?

1. Did you come to school by yourself today? 
2. Have you ever been late for school? 
3. Have you ever seen a musical at the theater? 
4. Did you help your friends today? 
5. Have you ever eaten popcorn at the movie theater? 
6. Have you ever made a birthday cake? 
7. Did you eat all your lunch yesterday? 
8. Have you ever played in a band? 
9. Have you ever played the harp? 
10. What did you do yesterday by yourself?
11. Which do you like: a comedy, a cartoon, or a thriller?
12. Did you say "Good morning" today?
13. Have you ever watched a sci-fi movie?
14. How was the weather yesterday?
15. Have you ever listened to jazz?

"Yes, I have!"

"You're right. Yes, I have. Good job!"

"Have you ever seen a musical at the theater?"

34 Look at other units. Ask more questions with *Have you ever...?*

"Have you ever been to the shopping mall by yourself?"

"Have you ever had a really good day?"

35 What did you enjoy in this unit? What do you want to know more about?

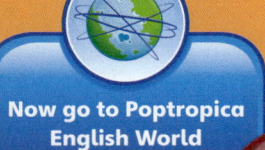

Now go to Poptropica English World

Lesson 10

Can use what I have learned in Unit 6

81

Review Units 5 and 6

1 Number. Then write.

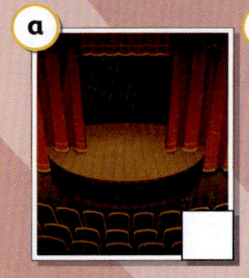

a   b   c   d   e   f

1 A king or queen lives here.
2 We can see actors here.
3 We can see a lot of fish here.
4 We can see paintings and dinosaurs here.
5 We can ride a roller coaster here.
6 We can jump into the water here.

_____
_____
_____
_____
_____
_____

2 Listen and match. Where will the girl go?

1 First   a aquarium
2 Second   b museum
3 Third   c circus
4 Fourth   d palace

3 Listen and write Y = Yes or N = No.

1   2   3   4

4 Unscramble. Then look at Activity 3 and circle T = True or F = False.

1 the / she / roller coaster / liked   T / F
2 playing / they / miniature golf / like / didn't   T / F
3 liked / she / Ferris wheel / the   T / F
4 bumper cars / like / the / he / didn't   T / F

Can talk about trips and attractions

5 Listen and number. Then write.

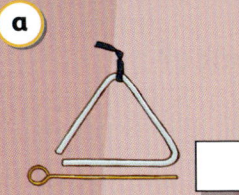

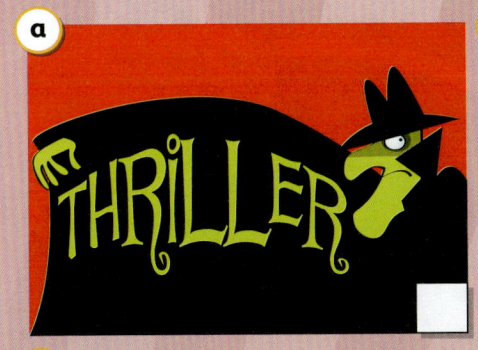

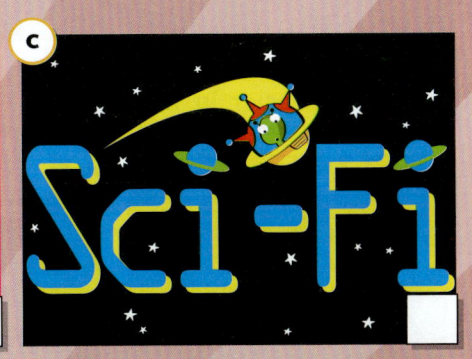

a. _____ b. _____ c. _____ d. _____ e. _____

6 Listen and number.

a. THRILLER   b. Romance   c. Sci-Fi
d. MUSICAL   e. CARTOON   f. comedy

7 Ask and answer.

1. What did you do yesterday?
2. Did you… last summer?
3. Did you… by yourself?
4. Have you ever…?

8 Complete the sentences.

1. Yesterday, I _____ by myself.
2. I have never _____.

Review Units 5 and 6   Can talk about the arts

7 Space

1 ⭐ Do you know the names in English of any things in space?

2 🎧 Listen and read. Where are Tom and Flo?

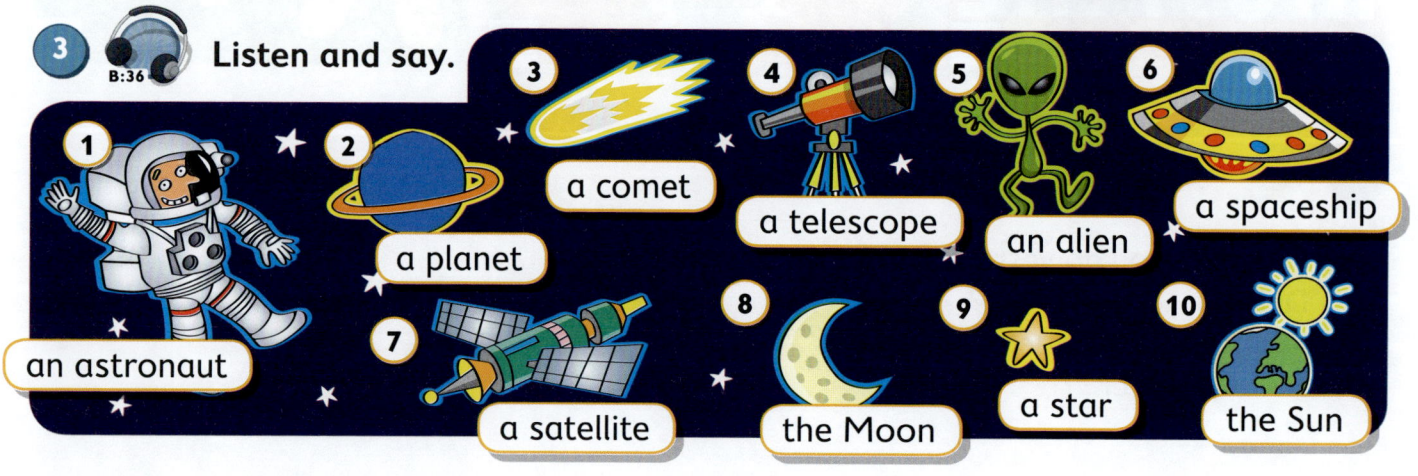

1 Felipe, why did you bring a telescope?
I like to watch the stars at night. It's much easier in the country.

2 Wow! What's that big red light?
Let me see. Where is it?

3 Here. It's amazing. Maybe it's a spaceship.

4 It isn't a spaceship. It's just a campfire on the hill.
Who is it?

5 It's Tom and Flo. Come on, let's go!

3 🎧 Listen and say.

1. an astronaut
2. a planet
3. a comet
4. a telescope
5. an alien
6. a spaceship
7. a satellite
8. the Moon
9. a star
10. the Sun

4 Look at Activity 3. Answer the questions.

1. What can you watch with a telescope?
2. Where is the astronaut?
3. Who travels in a spaceship?
4. What is around the planet?

Lesson 1

Can identify things in space

LOOK!

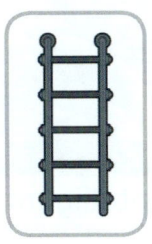

Who are they?	They're astronauts.
When did they come?	They came last night.
Where did they come from?	They came from the Moon.
How did they get here?	They came by spaceship.
Why are you looking at the sky?	I saw a flashing light.
What's that flashing light?	It's a spaceship.

5 Listen. Then circle.

1 Where was Sam in his dream?
2 Why was he there?
3 What was there inside the spaceship?

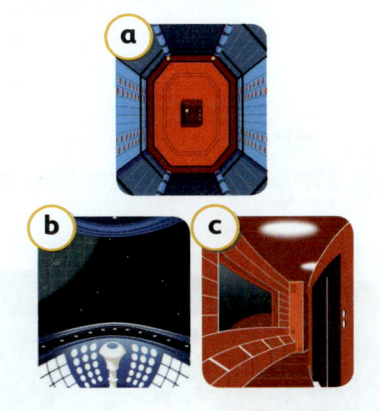

6 Listen again and write the question words.

> What   When   Where   Who   Why

1 _____ did you go to bed last night? I went to bed early, but I had a weird dream.
2 I went back to school late at night. _____ did you do that?
3 I went inside and I saw some strange people. _____ were they?
4 _____ was the spaceship? It was on the baseball field.
5 Cool! _____ did it look like? It was blue and white, and there were a lot of lights and buttons inside.

7 Ask and answer.

1 Who is your favorite teacher?
2 Why are you happy/tired/excited?
3 Where is your home?
4 What sports do you like?
5 When is your birthday?

Lesson 2 Can ask and answer using *How*, *What*, *When*, *Where*, *Who*, and *Why*   85

8 Listen and say. Then give examples.

1. complicated
2. amazing
3. frightening
4. intelligent
5. brilliant
6. important
7. fascinating
8. gorgeous

VOCABULARY

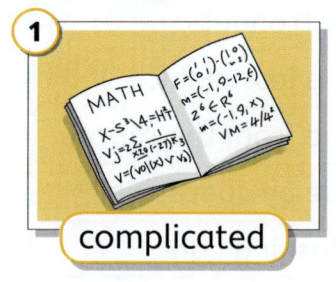

Snakes and high places are frightening.

Machines and rocket science are complicated.

9 Listen to the song and write.

SONG

Travel in space is ^{1} _____ exciting
Than travel on Earth below.
It's more ^{2} _____, too, and more ^{3} _____,
If you really want to know.
The question is – think about it,
Do ^{4} _____ live out there?
And if they do, are they more ^{5} _____
Than humans everywhere?
I don't know all the answers,
But one thing I know is true,
That the world is an ^{6} _____ place,
And it's just right for me and you, me and you.

10 Ask and answer.

1. What animal is frightening to you?
2. Who is the most important person in your country?
3. What do you think is the most complicated/most fascinating school subject?
4. Where is an amazing place in your country? Why is it amazing?

Lesson 3

Can identify and use descriptive words

SKILLS 7

LOOK!

Which telescope is more complicated?	The big telescope is more complicated than the small telescope.
Which telescope is the most complicated?	The big telescope is the most complicated.
Which telescope is less complicated?	The small telescope is less complicated than the big telescope.
Which telescope is the least complicated?	The small telescope is the least complicated.

11 Listen and check (✓). Then ask and answer.

1 a b
2 a b
3 a b
4 a b

12 Make sentences and say. Do you agree?

1 English / complicated / math
2 a thriller / frightening / a musical
3 cats / intelligent / dogs
4 sci-fi movies / interesting / romances
5 big snake / frightening
6 playing video games / important

13 Read and draw three things.

1 This one is the most frightening.
2 This one is the least complicated.
3 This one is the most amazing.

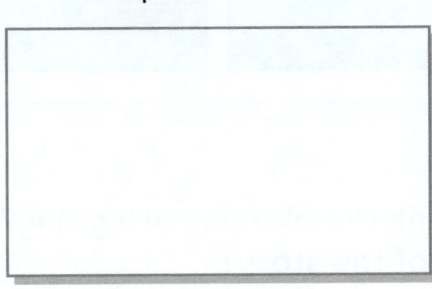

Lesson 4 — Can ask and answer about things using *more/less* and *most/least*

14. Talk about the pictures. Then listen and read.

STORY

1. ZEB AND DOT BUILT A MACHINE.
   "We're ready."
   "Finally! I can't wait!"

2. "This will work! Don't worry!"

3. "Wow! Come on, where are you?"

4. "What is that? A comet?"
   "I don't think so."
   "Come on!"

5. "Quick!"
   "They're going up!"

6. "Are they astronauts?"
   "Hmm, I wonder."
   "This is the most amazing adventure EVER!"

15. Where do you think the Martins are going? What can you see/hear from other parts of the story?

16 Match and make a summary.

1 Zeb and Dot are busy.
2 Dot is excited.
3 Zeb isn't worried.
4 A spaceship arrives.
5 Bella thinks the spaceship is a comet.
6 They get to the top of the mountain.

a He knows their machine will work.
b But the spaceship and the Martins have left.
c They are building a machine.
d AL doesn't agree with her.
e She can't wait for the spaceship to arrive.
f Dot and Zeb are very happy to see it!

17 Unscramble and write questions.

1 did / build / they / where / the / machine _____?
They built the machine on top of a mountain.
2 things / why / take / the / all / did / they _____?
Because they wanted to make a complicated machine.
3 the / who / Martins / are _____?
They are aliens from another planet.

18 Role-play the story.

19 Look at each picture and try to guess what it is. Use your imagination. Then share with a friend.

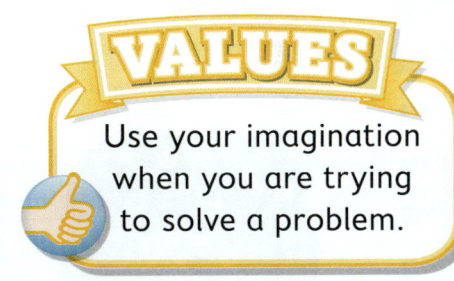

VALUES
Use your imagination when you are trying to solve a problem.

	1	2	3	4	5
Picture					
Your guess					
Your friend's guess					

What about Picture 1? Maybe it's a...

I think maybe it's a... or a...

HOME SCHOOL LINK Tell your family how you used your imagination to solve a problem.

Lesson 6 — Can understand details of a story / Can use my imagination to solve a problem — 89

20 Listen and read Connor's story. Then number the pictures.

The lost spaceship

1 One day in April last year, a spaceship landed in a field. It was only four o'clock in the morning, but the noise and the lights woke Jake up. He looked out of his bedroom window.

2 There was a strange object, like a round spaceship, in the field behind his house. A door opened at the bottom of the spaceship, and some strange people started walking out into the field.

3 They had large heads and small bodies, and they were green. Jake watched with his mouth open. "Am I dreaming?" he said. "Who are those people? Where are they from? What language do they speak?" he wondered. This was more exciting than any dream.

4 He put on his jeans and a T-shirt, went downstairs, opened the front door, and ran to the spaceship. His mom and dad were in bed…

Connor

21 Write questions that Jake could ask the aliens.

1 Who _____?
2 Where _____?
3 What _____?
4 Why _____?

22 Write the end of Connor's story.

_____
_____
_____

Lesson 7 — Can understand and write the end of a story

SCIENCE 7

23 ⭐ What do you know?

24 Read the facts. Number to match the questions to the answers.

Six Space Facts!

1 What color are stars?

2 Who was the first man in space?

3 When did the first men land on the Moon?

4 Where do astronauts sleep in space?

5 How do we know that life was once possible on Mars?

6 Is Saturn closer to the Sun than Jupiter?

a In 1969, the astronauts Neil Armstrong and Buzz Aldrin were the first men on the Moon. Armstrong said that it was "a small step for man but a giant leap for mankind."

b In 2011, scientists sent a special robot called the Curiosity Rover to Mars. In July 2014, the robot made an amazing discovery. Scientists now believe it is possible that there was life on Mars in the past.

c They can be different colors. Hot stars are blue, cool stars are red, and the Sun is yellow.

d In sleeping bags. The sleeping bags are tied to the wall! Sleeping in space is complicated because of gravity. It makes things float up if they aren't tied down.

e Yuri Gagarin was the first man in space. He went into space in 1961. He made a brave, brilliant leap into the dark. He went where no one else had ever gone before.

f No, it isn't. It's 1,426 million kilometers from the Sun, and Jupiter is 778 million kilometers from the Sun.

MINI PROJECT

SPACE FACTS POSTER

26 Create a poster with fascinating information about space.

- **Ideas** – Look at the space words in Activity 3 on page 84. Choose six that you are interested in.
- **Plan** – Find out some more information about the six space words you chose. Write notes about them.
- **Write** – Look at the model text. Write six questions and one or two facts for each. Draw/Stick some pictures.
- **Share** – Tell your classmate about your space facts poster.

25 🎧 Listen and check your answers. How many did you know?

B:47

Lesson 8   Can understand space facts / Can create a space facts poster   91

27 Look at the pictures and write the words.

| 1 _____ | 2 _____ | 3 _____ | 4 _____ |
| 5 _____ | 6 _____ | 7 _____ | 8 _____ |

28 Write. Then listen and check.

> amazing   brilliant   comets   complicated   frightening
> important   intelligent   planet   spaceships   telescope

Last night, I was looking at the night sky with my ¹_____. My dad is ²_____. He helped me set it up because it was a little ³_____. We looked at the Moon, many stars, and a ⁴_____ called Venus. It's ⁵_____ to see things which are so far away. My dad said that it's very ⁶_____ not to look directly at the Sun with a telescope. So, today I'm looking at a book about the Sun and space. The book has some interesting pictures of the Sun and ⁷_____. The picture of Saturn's rings is ⁸_____. Some people think space is ⁹_____. They think about going in ¹⁰_____ and that it may be dangerous, but I think it's very exciting.

29 Unscramble and write questions. Then ask and answer.

1 brilliant / is / a scientist / more / – a writer / who / or
   _____?

2 history / is / fascinating / more / what / – science / or
   _____?

3 – in the morning / least / when / tired / at night / are / you / or
   _____?

I CAN

I can identify things in space.
I can ask and answer using *How, What, When, Where, Who,* and *Why.*
I can create a space facts poster.

Lesson 9

30 Play. Use space words.

HAVE FUN 7

					T¹						
					E³						
					L³						
S¹	P³	A¹	C⁶	E¹							
					S²						
					C³						
					O¹						
					P³						
					E²						

	A	B	C	D	E	F	G	H	I	J	K	L	M
Points	1	3	3	4	1	5	3	4	1	8	7	3	5
	N	O	P	Q	R	S	T	U	V	W	X	Y	Z
Points	2	1	3	10	2	1	1	1	5	5	10	5	10

	Your words	Your points
1		
2		
3		
4		
5		
6		
7		
8		
9		
10		
	TOTAL	

How to play

1 Make a word.   **2** Write it on the board.
3 Check your points.   **4** Write your score.

🌙 = **2** x points for the letter

⭐ = **3** x points for the letter

31 ⭐ What did you enjoy in this unit? What do you want to know more about?

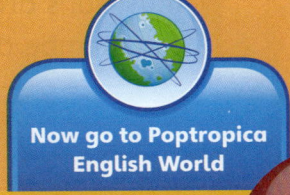

Now go to Poptropica English World

Lesson 10

Wider World 4
World instruments

1 ⭐ **What do you know?**

2 🗣 **Look at pictures a–c and make sentences.**

There's a man playing music.

a

b

3 🎧 **Listen and read. Then number the pictures in Activity 2.**

1 I live in Mali, Africa. Djembe drums are very famous in my country. People made djembe drums more than 1,500 years ago. These drums are made of hard wood and goat's skin. Sometimes there are beautiful pictures of animals or people on them, too. We like listening to the djembe drums and dancing. Today, people in Africa play these drums for special celebrations. Famous musicians around the world like playing the djembe drums, too.

Moussa, 11, Mali

2 I live in Buenos Aires, Argentina. People in my country play an instrument called the bandoneón. A bandoneón player pushes and pulls on the instrument to make beautiful music. It has square boxes at each end. The boxes are made of wood and have 71 buttons on them. Each button can play two different notes. The bandoneón is very difficult to play. It can take 10 years to learn. We play the bandoneón when people dance the tango. It's great music for dancing!

Marta, 11, Argentina

Wider World 4

Can understand texts about world instruments

C

4 Circle T = True or F = False.

1. Djembe drums are famous in (Argentina / Mali / Japan).
2. The boxes on a bandoneón are made of (metal / glass / wood).
3. Street singers use the (shamisen / djembe drum / bandoneón) to tell stories.
4. A shamisen has (six / four / three) strings.
5. People made the first djembe drum (40,000 / 1,500 / 2,000) years ago.
6. A (djembe drum / bandoneón / shamisen) has 71 buttons on it.

5 Ask and answer.

1. What instruments do people play in your country?
2. Can you play an instrument?
3. Which instrument do you want to learn?

3

I'm from Okinawa in Japan. A famous instrument in my country is the shamisen. It's like a guitar. It has a long, thin neck, but it only has three strings. People play it with a short piece of wood. Sometimes people sing while they play the shamisen. Street singers use the shamisen to tell stories. People use it in theater, too. Today, some Japanese rock bands also play the shamisen.

Takahiro, 12, Japan

YOUR TURN!

Make a list of some instruments and where they're from.

Djembe drums
– Africa
Shamisen
– ...

Find out about other instruments from around the world.

Wider World 4 — Can talk about instruments people play in my country — 95

8 The environment

1 ⭐ Do you know any ways to help the environment? What are the most important?

2 🎧 B:50 Listen and read. Why is Flo sad?

1
- It's the last day of camp. I'm sad.
- Come on! Let's clean up!

2
- What are you going to do?
- I'm going to pick up the trash.
- And I'm going to help Maria.

3
- I'm going to turn off the lights in the kitchen. Then I'm going to help Tom.
- Yes, I'm going to recycle the bottles.

4
- Are you going to help, Hannah?
- Well, you're all busy... I'm going to watch!

3 🎧 B:51 Listen and say.

1. recycle paper
2. recycle bottles
3. pick up trash
4. reuse plastic bags
5. turn off the lights
6. use public transportation

4 Look at Activity 3. What does your family do?

96 **Lesson 1**

Can identify ways to help the environment

LOOK!

Are you going to recycle paper?   Yes, **I am**.
No, **I'm not**. **I'm going to** recycle bottles.

5 Look at Activity 2. What are they going to do?

1 Maria and Flo are going to _____.
2 Felipe is _____.
3 Tom _____.
4 Hannah _____.

6 Listen and match. Then say.

Flo is going to have a big dinner with her family.

1    2    3

a    b    c

7 Look and find. Then say.

I'm going to turn off the TV.

1 five things to turn off
2 four things to recycle
3 five things to clean

Lesson 2

Can talk about things people are going to do

97

VOCABULARY

8 Read and match the actions to the pictures. Then listen and say.

1. save trees
2. save resources
3. keep the planet clean

a turn off the lights **b** reuse plastic bags **c** recycle bottles
d recycle paper **e** use public transportation **f** pick up trash

4. reduce waste
5. conserve energy
6. reduce pollution

SONG

9 Listen to the song and write.

What can you do to help save the Earth?
You can use public transportation and not always take a car.
There'll be less pollution; you can do your part to help save the Earth,
By cleaning up the air, cleaning up the air.
What other things can you do to help save the Earth?
1 _____ all waste paper, and 2 _____ some trees.
At home 3 _____ the lights, and in stores 4 _____ your bags.
5 _____ trash on the sidewalk.
Keep the planet 6 _____.
So, what's the most beautiful place in the world?
I'm not sure I can say, I really don't know.
The mountains, the oceans, the fields of green.
Let's take care of this planet and keep it clean!
Keep it clean, keep it clean.
Let's take care of this planet and keep it clean!

10 Share your ideas. What can you do to help?

1. conserve energy
2. keep your town clean
3. reduce waste
4. reduce pollution

Lesson 3

SKILLS 8

LOOK!

| What can you do to help? | I can use public transportation. |

If you reuse plastic bags, you'll reduce waste.

TIP!

I will = I'll / You will = You'll

He will = He'll / She will = She'll

They will = They'll / We will = We'll

11 Match. Then listen and check.

Way to help the environment

1 
2 
3 
4 
5 
6

How it saves the planet

a 
b 
c 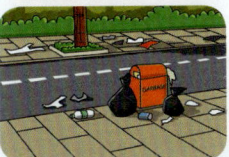
d 
e 
f

12 Look at Activity 11 and write.

1 If _____ , you'll _____ .
2 _____
3 _____
4 _____
5 _____
6 _____

Lesson 4   Can write about ways to help the environment using *If you… , you'll…*

13 **Talk about the pictures. Then listen and read.**

STORY

ON BOARD THE SPACESHIP

1 You aren't astronauts, you're aliens!
Yes, we just want to go home, to Mars.

2 Our ship broke down. We needed some important things.
What, like a saxophone? And a trash can of old food?

3 Yes. We used the saxophone to send a message to our people, and we recycle old food as biofuel.

4 We took the THD to time-travel here. But we need a space-time chip to get home.
I can help you... if you give us back our new THD.

5 Thank you!
You're welcome!
We'll get home safely now.
You're welcome!

6 Well, we have to go home now, too.
Yes, sir. Back to Bella's adventure camp, then.
Oh. I'm going to miss you guys!

14 **Why is the space-time chip important to the Martins? What does AL want? Why?**

Lesson 5

Can understand a simple story / Can discuss a story

15 Answer the questions.

1 Where are the Martins from?
_____

2 What do the Martins do that helps the environment?
_____

3 Where will Matt, Bella, and AL go next?
_____

16 Ask and answer.

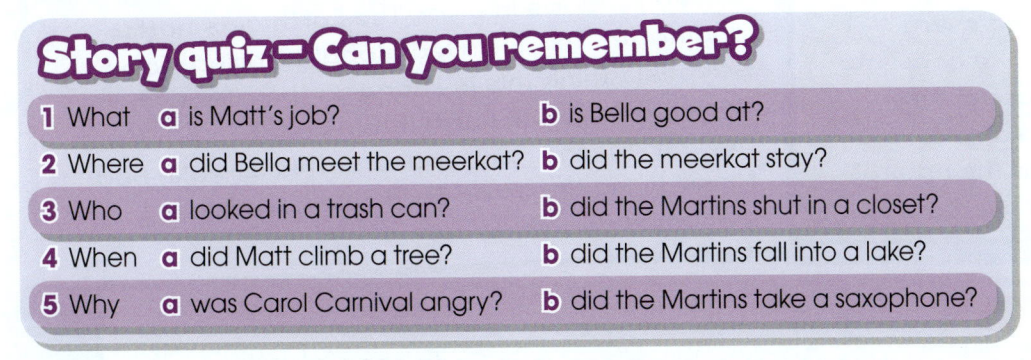

Story quiz – Can you remember?

1 What	a is Matt's job?	b is Bella good at?
2 Where	a did Bella meet the meerkat?	b did the meerkat stay?
3 Who	a looked in a trash can?	b did the Martins shut in a closet?
4 When	a did Matt climb a tree?	b did the Martins fall into a lake?
5 Why	a was Carol Carnival angry?	b did the Martins take a saxophone?

17 Role-play the story.

VALUES
Save our planet. Learn to save energy and keep the planet clean.

18 How good are you at protecting our planet? Take the test.

Check (✓) the right box.

	Never (0)	Sometimes (2)	Always (5)	Score
1 I put my trash in recycling bins.				
2 I turn off the lights to save electricity.				
3 I take very quick showers to save water.				
4 I often write on both sides of a sheet of paper.				
5 I reuse my own plastic bags at stores.				
6 I reduce pollution by riding a bike or walking.				

Your total score _____

0–12 points: You're not helping to save the planet. You have to change now!

13–26 points: You're helping to save the planet, but you can do more! Make an effort!

27–40 points: Congratulations! You're very good at helping the planet. Keep it up!

HOME SCHOOL LINK Tell your family about ways to save energy at home.

Lesson 6 — Can understand details of a story / Can assess how good I am at protecting the planet

19 Listen and read. Then number the pictures.

What are we doing to our planet?

1 Air Pollution

Air pollution has many causes. Factories, cars, trucks, and planes burn fuel and send poisonous gases into the air. These make us sick. Then, in some parts of the planet, large areas of forest are burned every year for farming. The smoke goes into the air, too. We need to use cleaner sources of energy, for example, solar energy, wind energy, and the natural force of the water in big rivers.

2 Global Warming

Have you ever been inside a car, parked in the sun? When the windows are closed, it gets hotter and hotter inside the car. The poisonous gases around the Earth are similar to the closed windows in a car. The Earth gets hotter and hotter. This is called global warming. Some scientists think this is changing the climate. In some parts of the Earth it rains a lot; in other parts it doesn't rain for years. This is really bad for all living things on Earth. We have to stop poisoning the air!

3 Tons of Trash

Billions of tons of trash are produced by humans every year. Soda cans, plastic bottles, and bags are a big problem. They accumulate on land and in rivers, streams, and oceans, and kill many ocean animals. We have to reduce the amount of plastic and metal we use, reuse what we can, and recycle the rest.

a   b   c

20 Read the text again. Write a cause of each problem.

1   Air pollution _____.
2   Global warming _____.
3   Too much trash _____.

21 Look at Activity 19 again and underline the solutions to each problem in the text.

Lesson 7

Can understand a text about environmental problems

22 ⭐ What do you know?

23 🎧 Listen and read. Then number the pictures.

GEOGRAPHY 8

Our Amazing World

1. The highest waterfall in the world is Angel Falls in Venezuela. It's 979 meters high.
2. Australia is the biggest island and the smallest continent in the world.
3. The Sahara desert in North Africa is the biggest desert in the world. The Atacama desert in Chile, South America, is probably the driest place in the world.
4. The Nile in Africa is the longest river in the world, but the Amazon River is a very close second. You can see the Nile in nine countries.
5. Mount Fuji is a very famous volcano in Japan. It's the highest mountain in Japan, too — it's 3,776 meters high.

24 Circle.

1. The highest waterfall in the world is in (Japan / Venezuela).
2. (The Nile / Mount Fuji) is in Japan.
3. The Atacama desert is the (driest / wettest) place in the world.
4. The biggest island in the world is (Japan / Australia).
5. Mount Fuji is (3,776 / 979) meters high.
6. You can see (the Nile / the Amazon river) in nine countries.

MINI PROJECT

25 Write about your amazing country. Create a fact poster.

- **Ideas** – Think about some amazing places.
- **Plan** – Choose five places to write about. Find out some more information about them.
- **Write** – Write one or two facts for each place. Draw/Stick some pictures.
- **Share** – Tell your classmate about your places.

Lesson 8 — Can understand texts about our amazing world / Can create a fact poster about my country

26 Circle.

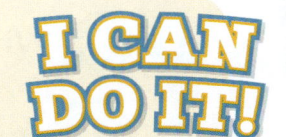

1. If you recycle (bottles / lights), you'll save (transportation / resources).
2. If you (reuse / pick up) trash, you'll keep the (energy / planet) clean.
3. If you turn (on / off) the lights, you'll (conserve / reuse) energy.
4. If you reuse (plastic / pollution), you'll reduce (water / waste).

27 Unscramble and write. Then match.

1. bottles / if / recycle / you / the
   _____
2. going / paper / I'm / to / recycle
   _____
3. I'm / plastic / going / bags / to / reuse
   _____
4. the / turn / lights / off / if / we
   _____
5. transportation / if / we / public / use
   _____

a   we'll conserve energy.

b   This will reduce waste.

c   I'll pick up the trash.

d   This will save trees.

e   we'll reduce pollution.

28 Look at the pictures in Activity 3. Then ask and answer.

What can you do to help the environment?

I can reuse plastic bags.

Are you going to recycle paper?

Yes, I am. What about you?

I CAN

I can talk about things people are going to do.
I can identify and talk about activities that help save the Earth.
I can create a fact poster about my country.

Lesson 9

29. **Play Os and Xs.**

I'm going to reuse plastic bags.

HAVE FUN

8

30. **Play Bingo.**

pick up trash
collect glass bottles
make compost
recycle paper
reuse plastic bags
recycle plastic bottles
turn off the lights
walk to school
use buses and trains

31. **Look at other units. Ask more questions with *Are you going to...?***

Are you going to see a movie this weekend?

Are you going to pass your test next week?

32. What did you enjoy in this unit? What do you want to know more about?

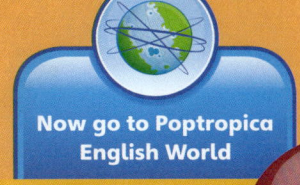

Now go to Poptropica English World

Lesson 10

Review Units 7 and 8

1 Write.

1. _____ is he?
He's an _____.

2. _____ did he go?
He went to the _____.

3. _____ did he go there?
He went by _____.

4. _____ is it?
It's a _____.

2 Write. Then ask a friend.

1. _____ is your birthday?
It's on...

2. _____ do you study English?
I study English because...

3 Look and check (✓).

1. Which is more complicated?
   a. 2×2=4
   b. 2X+3b²

2. Which is less frightening?
   a. Fun Farm
   b. Spy Shadows

3. Which is the least intelligent?
   a. 
   b.

4. Which is the most important?
   a. 
   b.

4 Listen and number the sentences in order.

a ☐ Are you going to help?
b ☐ OK, you can pick up trash at 3 p.m. Then I'll relax and save my energy.
c ☐ I need a break. If you give me 15 minutes, I'll help later.
d ☐ Great. I'm going to sit here and watch!
e ☐ I'm going to collect these old newspapers and recycle them.

5 Circle.

1 If you recycle (bottles / lights), you'll save (transportation / resources).
2 If you (reuse / pick up) trash, you'll keep the (energy / planet) clean.
3 If you use (plastic / public) transportation, you'll reduce (pollution / resources).
4 If you turn (on / off) the lights, you'll (conserve / reuse) energy.
5 If you reuse (plastic / pollution) bags, you'll reduce (water / waste).
6 If you (recycle / turn off) paper, you'll (reduce / save) trees.

6 Label the picture using the words in the box.

reuse   recycle   turn off   use

1 _____
2 _____
3 _____
4 _____

7 What can you do to help the environment where you live?

1 I can _____.
2 I'm going to _____.

Review Units 7 and 8   Can talk about ways to help the environment   107

Goodbye

1 🎧 C:03 Listen to the summary and number.

a At Adventure Camp

b On Future Island

c Home on Mars

2 Ask and answer.

1. What was your favorite scene in the story? Why?
2. Who was your favorite character in the story? Why?
3. When did you start to think that Dot and Zeb were aliens?
4. How did Bella and AL help Matt during the adventure?
5. Do you want to live on Future Island? Why?/Why not?

3 Which unit are these pictures from?

1 Unit ____   2 Unit ____   3 Unit ____   4 Unit ____

4 Who said this? Write.

1 "It's there – near the movie theater."   _____ Unit ____
2 "Good, I'm really hungry!"   _____ Unit ____
3 "… and it made terrible noises…"   _____ Unit ____
4 "What are you going to do?"   _____ Unit ____

5 Match the values to the things that they did.

1 Felipe planned to go on the water slide first at the amusement park.
2 They picked up trash and recycled bottles.
3 Felipe said, "Don't worry. I cooked a big stew for dinner."
4 They took compasses and a first-aid kit to their camp.

a Be positive about your day.
b Planning helps you do more things.
c Save our planet.
d Safety first.

6 Ask and answer.

1 What new things did you learn about nature in this book?
2 Which project was the most complicated?
3 Who was the most brilliant character or person in the book?
4 Which "Have Fun" page was the most fun to do?
5 What was your favorite song in this book? Can you sing it?

7 What was the most important thing your talk partners did that helped you learn well together?

_____
_____

Lesson 2

8 Write about your future. Ask a friend to read and comment.

In the future, I will _____
_____
_____
_____

"I've read this." Friend signs here: _____
Friend's comment: _____
_____
_____

9 Choose three friends or family members. Draw and write about them.

My _____

stick picture / draw here

1 _My mom is younger than my dad, but my sister is the youngest._
2 _____
3 _____
4 _____
5 _____
6 _____

Lesson 3 — Can use what I have learned

10 What is a famous food in your country? How do you make it? Draw a comic strip and write.

1 First, _____
   _____.

2 _____
   _____

3 _____
   _____

4 _____
   _____

11 Write four questions. Then ask three friends and ✓ or ✗.

Have you ever...?	Friend 1 Name: _____	Friend 2 Name: _____	Friend 3 Name: _____
1 been to another country			
2			
3			
4			
5			

12 Write words across that fit. Can you find 11 more words in this book?

```
          F
          U
          T
          U
          R
          E
          
          I
          S
      S T A R
          N
          D
```

Lesson 4 Can use what I have learned **111**

Wordlist

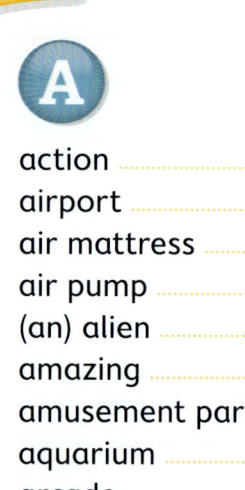

A

action	p. 72
airport	p. 38
air mattress	p. 12
air pump	p. 12
(an) alien	p. 84
amazing	p. 55
amusement park	p. 60
aquarium	p. 60
arcade	p. 38
(an) astronaut	p. 84

B

bank	p. 36
biggest	p. 26
bookstore	p. 38
botanical gardens	p. 60
brilliant	p. 86
bring my juice	p. 50

C

cartoon	p. 72
castanets	p. 74
castle	p. 36
cello	p. 74
cheetah	p. 24
circus	p. 60
clarinet	p. 74
coffee shop	p. 38
comedy	p. 72
(a) comet	p. 84
compass	p. 12
complicated	p. 86
conserve energy	p. 98
cover our heads	p. 14
curry	p. 48
cymbal	p. 74

D

drop the ball	p. 50
drums	p. 74
dumplings	p. 48

E

eat my lunch	p. 50
emu	p. 24

F

fascinating	p. 86
fastest	p. 26
feel	p. 10
first-aid kit	p. 12
fish and chips	p. 48
flashlight	p. 12
frightening	p. 86

G

go on the bumper cars	p. 62
go on the paddle boats	p. 62
go on the pirate ship	p. 62
go on the water slide	p. 62
gorgeous	p. 86

H

harmonica	p. 74
harp	p. 74
heaviest	p. 26
hospital	p. 38

I

important	p. 86
intelligent	p. 86

J

K

keep out the rain	p. 14
keep the planet clean	p. 98
koala	p. 24

L

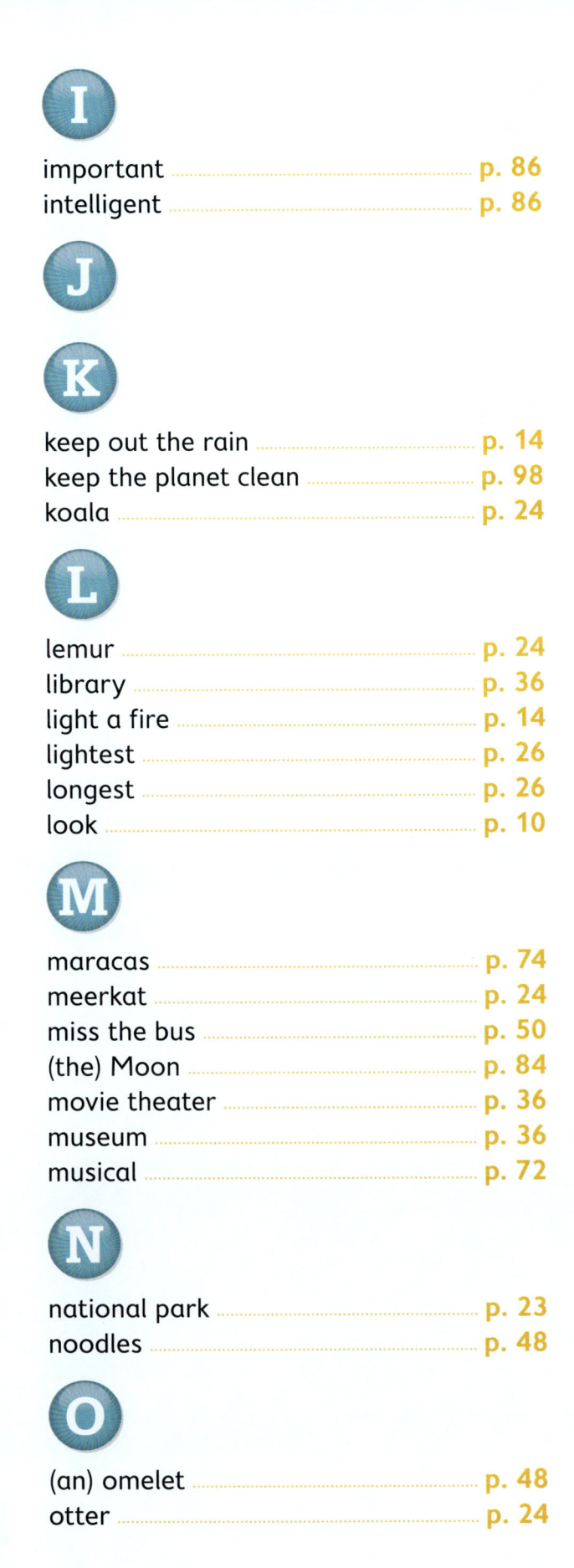

lemur	p. 24
library	p. 36
light a fire	p. 14
lightest	p. 26
longest	p. 26
look	p. 10

M

maracas	p. 74
meerkat	p. 24
miss the bus	p. 50
(the) Moon	p. 84
movie theater	p. 36
museum	p. 36
musical	p. 72

N

national park	p. 23
noodles	p. 48

O

(an) omelet	p. 48
otter	p. 24

P

pack my bag	p. 50
paella	p. 48
palace	p. 60
panther	p. 24
park	p. 36
pass a test	p. 50
pegs	p. 12
pharmacy	p. 36
pick up trash	pp. 96, 98
pitch the tent	p. 14
(a) planet	p. 84
play miniature golf	p. 62
poles	p. 12
put in the pegs	p. 14

Q

R

read a compass	p. 14
recycle bottles	pp. 96, 98
recycle paper	pp. 96, 98
reduce pollution	p. 98
reduce waste	p. 98
reuse plastic bags	pp. 96, 98
rhino	p. 24
rice and beans	p. 48
ride the Ferris wheel	p. 62
ride the roller coaster	p. 62
romance	p. 72

S

(a) satellite	p. 84
save resources	p. 98
save trees	p. 98
saxophone	p. 74
sci-fi	p. 72
scorpion	p. 24
sea turtle	p. 24

seal .... p. 24
set up the bed .... p. 14
shopping mall .... p. 36
shortest .... p. 26
sleeping bag .... p. 12
slowest .... p. 26
smallest .... p. 26
smell .... p. 10
sound .... p. 10
soup .... p. 48
spaghetti .... p. 48
(a) spaceship .... p. 84
(a) star .... p. 84
station .... p. 38
stew .... p. 48
(the) Sun .... p. 84
supermarket .... p. 36
sushi .... p. 48

T

take down the tent .... p. 14
tallest .... p. 26
tambourine .... p. 74
taste .... p. 10
(a) telescope .... p. 84
tent .... p. 12
theater .... p. 60
thriller .... p. 72
tiger .... p. 24
triangle .... p. 74
turn off the lights .... pp. 96, 98

U

use public transportation ...... pp. 96, 98

V

W

water park .... p. 60
western .... p. 72
whale .... p. 24

X

Y

Z

Verb list

Present	Past	Past Participle
act	acted	acted
agree	agreed	agreed
be: am/is/are	was/were	been
believe	believed	believed
beat	beat	beaten
blush	blushed	blushed
borrow	borrowed	borrowed
break	broke	broken
bring	brought	brought
brush	brushed	brushed
build	built	built
burn	burned	burned
buy	bought	bought
call	called	called
catch	caught	caught
chat	chatted	chatted
check	checked	checked
choose	chosen	chosen

Present	Past	Past Participle
clean	cleaned	cleaned
climb	climbed	climbed
clip	clipped	clipped
close	closed	closed
collect	collected	collected
comb	combed	combed
come	came	come
complain	complained	complained
complete	completed	completed
cost	cost	cost
count	counted	counted
cry	cried	cried
cut	cut	cut
dance	danced	danced
design	designed	designed
dig	dug	dug
do	did	done
download	downloaded	downloaded

Present	Past	Past Participle
draw	drew	drawn
dress	dressed	dressed
drink	drank	drunk
dry	dried	dried
dust	dusted	dusted
eat	ate	eaten
empty	emptied	emptied
explain	explained	explained
fail	failed	failed
fall	fell	fallen
feed	fed	fed
feel	felt	felt
find	found	found
finish	finished	finished
fix	fixed	fixed
floss	flossed	flossed
fly	flew	flown
follow	followed	followed
forget	forgot	forgotten
frown	frowned	frowned
get	got	gotten

Present	Past	Past Participle
give	gave	given
go	went	gone
hang	hung	hung
has/have	had	had
hear	heard	heard
help	helped	helped
hide	hid	hid
hit	hit	hit
install	installed	installed
join	joined	joined
jump	jumped	jumped
know	knew	known
laugh	laughed	laughed
lean	leaned	leaned
learn	learned	learned
leave	left	left
listen	listened	listened
live	lived	lived
look	looked	looked
lose	lost	lost
mail	mailed	mailed

Present	Past	Past Participle
make	made	made
meet	met	met
memorize	memorized	memorized
miss	missed	missed
mop	mopped	mopped
move	moved	moved
open	opened	opened
pack	packed	packed
paint	painted	painted
pass	passed	passed
pay	paid	paid
photograph	photographed	photographed
play	played	played
practice	practiced	practiced
prepare	prepared	prepared
print	printed	printed
pull	pulled	pulled
pump	pumped	pumped
push	pushed	pushed
put	put	put
rake	raked	raked

Present	Past	Past Participle
read	read	read
rent	rented	rented
rescue	rescued	rescued
rest	rested	rested
return	returned	returned
ride	rode	ridden
ring	rang	rung
roast	roasted	roasted
run	ran	run
say	said	said
search	searched	searched
see	saw	seen
sell	sold	sold
send	sent	sent
set	set	set
shake	shook	shaken
shoot	shot	shot
show	showed	shown
sign	signed	signed
sing	sang	sung
sit	sat	sat

Present	Past	Past Participle
skate	skated	skated
sleep	slept	slept
solve	solved	solved
stay	stayed	stayed
study	studied	studied
surf	surfed	surfed
sweat	sweated	sweated
sweep	swept	swept
swim	swam	swum
take	took	taken
talk	talked	talked
tell	told	told
text	texted	texted
think	thought	thought
throw	threw	thrown
tidy	tidied	tidied
tie	tied	tied
touch	touched	touched
trade	traded	traded

Present	Past	Past Participle
turn	turned	turned
use	used	used
visit	visited	visited
wait	waited	waited
walk	walked	walked
warm	warmed	warmed
wash	washed	washed
watch	watched	watched
water	watered	watered
wear	wore	worn
weed	weeded	weeded
whistle	whistled	whistled
win	won	won
worry	worried	worried
wrap	wrapped	wrapped
write	wrote	written
yawn	yawned	yawned
yell	yelled	yelled

Acknowledgments

The Publishers would like to thank the following teachers for their suggestions and comments on this course:
Nurhan Deniz, Alejandra Juarez, Lara Ozer, Cynthia Xu, Basia Zarzycka, Jamie Zhang

Jennifer Dobson, Anabel Higuera Gonzalez, Honorata Klosak, Dr Marianne Nikolov, Regina Ramalho

Hilda Martinez, Xochitl Arvizu, Tim Budden , Tina Chen, Betty Deng, Aaron Jolly, Dr. Nam-Joon Kang, Dr. Wonkey Lee, Wenxin Liang, Ann Mayeda, Wade O. Nichols

Asako Abe, JiEun Ahn, Nubia Isabel Albarracín, José Antonio Aranda Fuentes, Juritza Ardila, María del Carmen Ávila Tapia, Ernestina Baena, Marisela Bautista, Carmen Bautista, Norma Verónica Blanco, Suzette Bradford, Rose Brisbane, María Ernestina Bueno Rodríguez, María del Rosario Camargo Gómez, Maira Cantillo, Betsabé Cárdenas, María Cristina Castañeda, Carol Chen, Carrie Chen, Alice Chio, Tina Cho, Vicky Chung, Marcela Correa, Rosalinda Ponce de Leon, Betty Deng, Rhiannon Doherty, Esther Domínguez, Elizabeth Domínguez, Ren Dongmei, Gerardo Fernández, Catherine Gillis, Lois Gu, SoRa Han, Michelle He, María del Carmen Hernández, Suh Heui, Ryan Hillstead, JoJo Hong, Cindy Huang, Mie Inoue, Chiami Inoue, SoYun Jeong, Verónica Jiménez, Qi Jing, Sunshui Jing, Maiko Kainuma, YoungJin Kang, Chisato Kariya, Yoko Kato, Eriko Kawada, Sanae Kawamoto, Sarah Ker, Sheely Ker, Hyomin Kim, Lee Knight, Akiyo Kumazawa, JinJu Lee, Eunchae Lee, Jin-Yi Lee, Sharlene Liao, Yu Ya Link, Marcela Marluchi, Hilda Martínez Rosal, Alejandro Mateos Chávez, Cristina Medina Gómez, Bertha Elsi Méndez, Luz del Carmen Mercado, Ana Morales, Ana Estela Morales, Zita Morales Cruz, Shinano Murata, Junko Nishikawa, Sawako Ogawa, Ikuko Okada, Hiroko Okuno, Tomomi Owaki, Sayil Palacio Trejo, Rosa Lilia Paniagua, MiSook Park, SeonJeong Park, JoonYong Park, María Eugenia Pastrana, Silvia Santana Paulino, Dulce María Pineda, Rosalinda Ponce de León, Liliana Porras, María Elena Portugal, Yazmín Reyes, Diana Rivas Aguilar, Rosa Rivera Espinoza, Nayelli Guadalupe Rivera Martínez, Araceli Rivero Martínez, David Robin, Angélica Rodríguez, Leticia Santacruz Rodríguez, Silvia Santana Paulino, Kate Sato, Cassie Savoie, Mark Savoie, Yuki Scott, Yoshiko Shimoto, Jeehye Shin, MiYoung Song, Lisa Styles, Laura Sutton, Mayumi Tabuchi, Takako Takagi, Miriam Talonia, Yoshiko Tanaka, María Isabel Tenorio, Chioko Terui, José Francisco Trenado, Yasuko Tsujimoto, Elmer Usaguen, Hiroko Usami, Michael Valentine, José Javier Vargas, Nubia Margot Vargas, Guadalupe Vázquez, Norma Velázquez Gutiérrez, Ruth Marina Venegas, María Martha Villegas Rodríguez, Heidi Wang, Tomiko Watanabe, Jamie Wells, Susan Wu, Junko Yamaguchi, Dai Yang, Judy Yao, Yo Yo, Sally Yu, Mary Zhou, Rose Zhuang